# Joyful Noise

*by*

# Tim Slover

D0760436

# SAMUEL FRENCH, INC.

45 WEST 25TH STREET    NEW YORK 10010
7623 SUNSET BOULEVARD    HOLLYWOOD 90046
*LONDON*      *TORONTO*

ISBN 0 573 62759 2          Printed in U.S.A.          # 12911

# IMPORTANT BILLING AND CREDIT REQUIREMENTS

All producers of JOYFUL NOISE *must* give credit to the Author of the Play in all programs distributed in connection with performances of the Play and in all instances in which the title of the Play appears for purposes of advertising, publicizing or otherwise exploiting the Play and/ or a production. The name of the Author *must* also appear on a separate line, on which no other name appears, immediately following the title, and *must* appear in size of type not less than fifty percent the size of the title type.

# CHARACTERS:

**SUSANNAH CIBBER**
26-28, Singing actress, formerly of Drury Lane Theatre

**CHARLES JENNENS**
40-42, Squire of Gospel, librettist of *Messiah*

**GEORGE FREDERICK HANDEL**
55-57, Composer

**JOHN CHRISTOPHER SMITH**
47-49, Business manager, amanuensis for Handel

**KITTY CLIVE**
30-32, Singing actress, Drury Lane Theatre

**MARY PENDARVES**
41-43, Music patron

**GEORGE II**
57-59, King of England

**BISHOP HENRY EGERTON**
35-37, Clerk of the Closet for the Royal Household

The action of the play is set in and around London and Leicestershire, 1741-1743.

## NOTE

Scenes are meant to move from one to the other without pauses or blackouts. Set pieces should reflect this idea: generic enough to be shared across locations while possessive of a period look.


## A NOTE ON MUSIC

There is a prerecorded CD available which contains specially arranged instrumental accompaniments to the abbreviated anthem sung by Susannah in Act I, scene I (sheet music also available), and to the abbreviated *Messiah* Overture and arias sung by Susannah and Kitty in Act II, scene 9, as well as both instrumental-only and instrumental-choral accompaniments to the Hallelujah Chorus sung in Act II, scenes 9 and 10. A detailed sound-plot is supplied with the CD.

Samuel French, Inc. can supply *amateurs* with the prerecorded CD upon receipt of the following:
1) $25.00 refundable deposit on return of the material in good condition.
2) A $10.00 non-returnable rental fee.
3) A music royalty fee of $25.00 for the first performance, $20.00 for each subsequent performance.

Fees for stock performances upon application.

Other music is mentioned in the script, such as excerpts from Handel's Rinaldo, Queen Caroline's Funeral Anthem. These may be obtained from existing recordings, provided that copyright laws are observed. It is the author's intention that all music used in the play be composed by Handel.

*Make a joyful noise unto God, all ye lands.*
                                — Psalm 66


*The two most fascinating subjects in the universe
are sex and the Eighteenth Century.*
                                — Brigid Brophy,
                                *Don't Never Forget*

# ACT I

### Scene One
*Private room at Gopsal, Leicestershire*
*Susannah Cibber's Lodgings, London*
*Handel's Salon, Brook Street, February 1741*

*(A light on SUSANNAH CIBBER, 26, beautiful, frail. Behind her, for the moment out of sight, is a chair and a dress box tied up with cord. SUSANNAH is standing as though at the beginning of a recital performance. She is radiantly happy, exhilarated, popular, and successful. Incongruously, she holds a baby, wrapped in a blanket. Applause begins, and she acknowledges it with a deep, theatrical bow. Then she joyfully begins to sing Handel's anthem "Sing Unto God.")*

SUSANNAH.
"Blessed are all they that fear the Lord:
O well is thee, and happy shalt thou be."
*(Something goes wrong. Hands snatch the baby from her suddenly.)*
Molly! *(Now she is confused, but she quickly returns to her performance exhilaration and begins the song again.)*
"Blessed are all they that fear the Lord —"

*(Just as suddenly her dress is pulled away from her, leaving her standing in night dress. Laughter erupts around her. She stands, silent and ashamed, hearing the judgment of an unseen voice, which silences the laughter.)*

VOICE. *(Recorded)* Mrs. Cibber. Sit down. *(A chair is suddenly and loudly placed on the floor behind her, and she sits in it.)* Members of the jury, before you retire to deliberate this case, let me state clearly the opinion of the Solicitor-General. The crime of adultery has been clearly proved.

7

*(Crossfade to CHARLES JENNENS, 40. He is alone at a table upon which a thin manuscript sits with paper and string, ready to be tied up and posted. He is meticulous, insensitive, and extremely religious. He holds up the manuscript, pages through it, puts it down, leaves briefly.)*
*(Crossfade to GEORGE FREDERICK HANDEL, 55. He is heavy without being lugubrious, with a slight, pleasing German accent. He is putting the final touches on his dress, for he is going out. He carries a full-bottomed wig.)*

HANDEL. Smith! Smith, where are you?
SMITH. *(Off)* Just coming, Herr Handel.
HANDEL. Come in, will you? Always I have trouble with the neck cravat. *(JOHN CHRISTOPHER SMITH, 47, comes in. He is Handel's financial manager and amanuensis, a man of quiet efficiency.)* Ah. Will you help, please?

*(SMITH obliges. Crossfade to SUSANNAH. Her foregoing action was a dream, and she is still caught up in its vivid imagery. Now she speaks simultaneously with the offstage Voice, though perhaps she does not get out every word as she relives this horror.)*

VOICE/SUSANNAH. Doubtless, members of the jury, you are wondering at the suitability of allowing the bastard child to remain with the adulterous mother. What father, no matter how sinful, would wish that fate to befall his offspring?

*(She takes out a straight razor from her bag. She puts her arm down on the tied-up box, wrist up. Now she makes her decision: what will she cut, her wrist, or the cord?)*

SMITH. I'm not your valet, you know, Handel. Where's Le Blond?
HANDEL. Dozing, I think. So. Smith. The last night of the season. I think I will play the organ at the interval.
SMITH. Well, it isn't fair you've had to cut the season short.

*(SUSANNAH makes her decision and cuts the cords of the box. She opens it and removes a new gown, which she holds up to inspect. Back to SMITH and HANDEL:)*

SMITH. I call it dashed unfair. There. You have a tied cravat.

HANDEL. Will Walsh publish the score?

SMITH. Ah. Well, regrettably, as this particular opera hasn't taken with the town ...

HANDEL. Yes. What am I thinking? No one wishes to publish a disaster.

*(Back to JENNENS, who returns with a smoking censer. He crosses himself, censes the manuscript. He writes a brief letter.)*

JENNENS. My dear Handel. I hope I shall persuade you to set another scripture collection I have made for you. Indeed, I hope you will lay out your whole genius and skill upon it. Looking forward to an early reply, I have the honor to remain very sincerely yours, Charles Jennens, Esquire. *(He looks up.)* Now write some good music for it, you cantankerous, old German bear.

### Scene Two
#### *Offstage Dressing Area, Drury Lane Theatre*
#### *February 10, evening*

*(JENNENS exits, leaving his table, which now becomes a dressing-room table for KITTY CLIVE, 30, who will enter in a moment. SUSANNAH stands waiting, wearing the dress she removed from the box.)*

KITTY. *(Off)* "Cassio, walk hereabout; If I do find him fit, I'll move your suit —" *(She enters as she finishes her line and moves directly to the table to start a costume change. Also pretty, she is high-spirited, cocksure, and extremely tough. Her dislike for – and fear of – Susannah is intense.)* " — and seek to effect it to my uttermost." Bloody hell, I hate this bleedin' *Othello!* There's not a laugh in the whole rotten play!

SUSANNAH. *(Behind her.)* Hello, Mrs. Clive.

KITTY. *(Not looking.)* No one's allowed backstage at the interval.

SUSANNAH. Kitty.

KITTY. *(Turning to see who it is.)* Mrs. Cibber!

SUSANNAH. Yes, it's Susannah.

KITTY. How'd you get in here?

SUSANNAH. Fleetwood let me in. I've just come to town.

KITTY. Lord, it's been ages.

SUSANNAH. You're looking splendid.

KITTY. Am I? Even in this get-up? You're just flattering.

SUSANNAH. No, really.

KITTY. Well, it would be unbecoming to argue. I hope you'll excuse me, though, Mrs. Cibber. I've me costume to change.

SUSANNAH. *(Seeing a chance to ingratiate herself.)* Oh, let me help.

KITTY. Aren't you nice?

SUSANNAH. You're playing like an angel out there, Kitty.

KITTY. Am I?

SUSANNAH. Oh, yes.

KITTY. It's my first tragical role, you know.

SUSANNAH. No! I would never have guessed.

KITTY. I don't like it all that bleedin' much. Do you know I get smothered? At the end?

SUSANNAH. I believe all Desdemonas do.

KITTY. What sort of death is that for a leading actress? Don't none of these suffering types die from something pretty and delicate?'

SUSANNAH. I think not many.

KITTY. Of course, that was more your line, wasn't it? All that pining and pious sighing you used to call acting! God's my life, it didn't matter what role you was assigned: You played 'em all as the Virgin Mary.

SUSANNAH. You'll die beautifully, I'm sure. I can't wait to watch.

KITTY. *(A bit suspicious.)* Why are you here, Mrs. Cibber?

SUSANNAH. Well, I've decided to go back on the stage.

KITTY. After three years? Where? Here?

SUSANNAH. I understand Fleetwood's putting on *The Conscious Lovers*.

KITTY. Why would anyone want to come back to Dreary Lane Theatre? I'm sick to death of it, I can tell you.

SUSANNAH. He'll need someone to play Indiana.

KITTY. I'm off to do opera parts with Handel. I'm seeing him tomorrow. He can't wait to hear me sing.

SUSANNAH. You have influence here. I thought —

KITTY. Indiana is Hannah Pritchard's role now. Are you going to start filching from her, too?

SUSANNAH. What do you mean?

KITTY. Lord, hark at her. Butter wouldn't melt.

SUSANNAH. Would you speak to Fleetwood for me?

KITTY. That's bloody likely. After the injuries you done me.

SUSANNAH. I never meant to injure you, Kitty. I swear.

KITTY. Go ahead and swear! You stole parts from me, Mrs. Cibber. That's what I call injury.

SUSANNAH. No —

KITTY. You did!

SUSANNAH. It was Theophilus —

KITTY. It was you *and* your filthy husband!

SUSANNAH. — And it was years ago.

KITTY. Three. And it's taken me all three to get 'em back.

SUSANNAH. Just help me to some small part, Kitty.

KITTY. Small part? That's how you always bleedin' begin.

SUSANNAH. Please.

KITTY. I must ask you to leave me theatre now, Mrs. Cibber.

SUSANNAH. It's for Molly.

KITTY. Are you going to leave?

SUSANNAH. I can't. Not until you help me.

KITTY. Really? Aren't you brave? Alright then, tell me. What was it about William Sloper that first set you groaning for him?

SUSANNAH. What?

KITTY. Oh, he was handsomer than your husband, I'll grant you, but then a Kennington hog's handsomer than Theophilus Cibber! Was it the money? Or was it just a tickle in your thighs?

SUSANNAH. Please, Kitty —

KITTY. And how goes the sale of your book, Mrs. Cibber? Still doing well, is it?

SUSANNAH. It was never my book. You know that.

KITTY. There you are, on page after page, naked as seven devils for all the gentlemen to peer at. Wait, I believe I've still got some of it memorized: "He took her on his knees, lifted up her clothes and took down his breeches, took his privy member in his hand and —"

SUSANNAH. *(Covers her ears.)* Stop! For pity's sake, stop! How can you be so cruel?

KITTY. Oh, I can be lots of things, Mrs. Cibber. I've got range. Watch. *(All sweetness now.)* How is your daughter, dear? How is little Molly? She must be, what, three now? *(Suddenly sticking the knife in.)* Is that old enough to be proud of her mother? There. Had enough? Can I get back to bloody *Othello*? Let me be clear as glass: you'll never get back onstage if Catherine Clive has anything to say about it. And I do.

*(She exits. To SUSANNAH, these exchanges have been emotional body blows. Words from her trial come back into her mind.)*

VOICE. *(Recorded)* Squire Sloper is a young country gentleman, unused to the immoral ways of the town. But Susannah Cibber is another sort of person. She is theatrical; she is of the town.

*(MARY PENDARVES appears, 41, a beautiful, well-dressed, and kindly woman. Occasionally she seems a bit batty, but this is a pose. At the moment, she has come looking for KITTY, but sees SUSANNAH instead. She dislikes intensely every moment she must stay at Drury Lane Theatre.)*

MARY. Young woman? I do beg your pardon. I'm looking for a Mrs. Catherine Clive. Are you, by any chance, she? *(No response from SUSANNAH.)* I have a message for her. Can you tell me where she may be?

SUSANNAH. No.

MARY. Perhaps you would be so good as to give her this? *(Proffers a piece of paper.)* I really cannot stay here.

SUSANNAH. I ... don't know her.

MARY. Oh — *(Searches for the right word.)* — fiddle! You see, she's not to come see the Master. He'll not hear her sing tomorrow. If she comes along and pesters him, he'll explode like a Chinese firework.

SUSANNAH. The Master?

MARY. Herr Handel. His newest opera, you know, is failing. Despite its wit. Despite its exquisite beauty. Despite, despite. Tonight is its last performance.

SUSANNAH. You are acquainted with Mr. Handel?

MARY. I have that honor. Can you not help me find the Clive woman?

SUSANNAH. I'm sorry. Do you know him well?

MARY. Oh, drat! One tries not to swear, being a Christian and of quality, but, well, drat. Ah well, having failed in my task, I shall now take a hansom to Lincoln's Inn Fields to applaud the final act.

SUSANNAH. May I come with you?

MARY. This is abrupt. You wish to hear the strains of England's Orpheus?

SUSANNAH. It's forward of me, I know.

*(MARY examines SUSANNAH for a moment.)*

MARY. Not at all. You are distressed. One doesn't mean to observe, but one does. Yes. You come with me. See true greatness on the stage. It will tonic you something wonderful. "For when Orpheus plucks his tunéd string / Then art no less than nature sings." The couplet is my own.

SUSANNAH. Is it?

MARY. Introductions: I am Mrs. Mary Pendarves, wife to the sainted Mr. Pendarves, now deceased. And you are?

SUSANNAH. I'm ... Miss Archer.

MARY. Delighted. And now, Miss Archer, shall we go and hear the music of the Master?

### Scene Three
Onstage, Lincoln's Inn Fields Theater
The same night

*(As SUSANNAH and MARY exit, meager applause and rather perfunctory cries of "Handel!" are heard, as he comes onstage. He raises a hand for quiet, the applause tails off.)*

HANDEL. Thank you for coming to my opera tonight. I hope you liked it. *(Peering into the audience.)* Those of you who came, I think, found you were not crowded. You had plenty of room for your arms to rest and to carry on your fascinating conversations with one another, yes? Good. Tonight marks the close of this season's operas here at Lincoln's Inn Fields, which is my twenty-seventh since I came to your pleasant London. Thank you as always for your kind patronage. *(He bows. A smattering of applause. This is the conclusion of his speech. He bows and starts to leave, then changes his mind.)* And if you did not come so much this year as in other seasons, I am sure it was because the town is now so crowded with other entertainments. There is, for instance, the destruction of Shakespeare which goes on nightly at Drury Lane Theatre, and this you must see, yes? Oh, and the other *music* — which is so good, it takes the breath away. Over at the Haymarket, Madame Sallé dances in French bloomers to the exquisite music of Porpora. No matter that Porpora's music goes la la la la la all in one note; there are still, after all, the bloomers to attend to. *(Peers into the audience, sees that some are leaving.)* Wait, don't go! I have more to say! What has happened to the tastes of the town? Is it entirely filled now with coarse buffoons who wish only for dancing girls and bad music? No, don't go! Listen! *Deidamia* is the fortieth opera I have composed for you. It is not, I admit, so good as my *Imeneo* last November or as *Jove in Argo,* which also you did not attend. But remember this: it was still a Handel opera! Compared with all the other musical trash in this town, it is the songs of angels! I will tell you what I think. This town is no longer good enough for an opera by George Frederick Handel! *(SMITH comes on to usher HANDEL offstage, gently but forcefully.)* Ah, Smith! There you are. *(Resisting)* Wait, I have more to say to the town! *(Back to the audience.)* You are ungrateful! And you would not recognize music talent if it fell on you like slops from a second-story window!

SMITH. My dear Handel, no one marks you.

HANDEL. *(Passion spent.)* What?

SMITH. They have all left the theatre, you see.

HANDEL. Oh. Yes.

SMITH. Let's go home.

HANDEL. Yes. Let's go home.

*(They slowly leave, SMITH guiding.)*

### Scene Four
*Privy Chamber, St. James's Palace*
*The same night*

*(GEORGE II, 57, enters, being talked at by BISHOP HENRY EGERTON, 35. The King is passionate, volatile, and though not educated, intelligent enough. His German accent is about as noticeable as HANDEL'S. EGERTON is Bishop of Hereford, Clerk of the Closet in the Royal Household, and, though educated, not particularly flexible of mind.)*

GEORGE II. You want something, Bishop, but as usual you make it as hard to understand as possible.

EGERTON. What I am trying to say is, they call ours an age of enlightenment, sir, but, really, in the eyes of God, the former age was better illuminated by the light of the gospel.

GEORGE II. Are you saying that the reign of the House of Hanover — my family's reign — is less enlightened than the reign of the House of Stuart?

EGERTON. I quite see your point, your Majesty. Of course.

GEORGE II. Of course, what?

EGERTON. Of course not.

GEORGE II. Thank you.

EGERTON. Let me approach this in a different way, if I might. John Locke wrote —

GEORGE II. Who?

EGERTON. John Locke. The English political philosopher.

GEORGE II. *Ja, ja.*

EGERTON. Locke wrote that religion is a voluntary society of persons meeting together to worship God.

GEORGE II. So? This is good. Let them meet.

EGERTON. Well, yes, this is good in its way. And Parliament lets them. But, well …

GEORGE II. Well, what, Bishop!? This is growing tiresome. And it is rather late.

EGERTON. Well, sir, Locke was a Deist.

GEORGE II. So? Does the Church not allow a man to be a beeist?

EGERTON. I beg your pardon?

GEORGE II. So he kept bees. So what?

EGERTON. Oh, no, no your Majesty. You've misunder —, I have mis-spoken. John Locke was not a beeist. He did not keep bees. At least, I have not read that he did. Though, in truth, I have not read that he did not. Well, this could be researched. No, what I'm saying is that Locke was — also a — Deist. He believed that people may worship whatever and however they choose.

GEORGE II. Ah, I see. And this is bad for you.

EGERTON. Bad for me?

GEORGE II. Of course. Fewer people at St. Paul's Cathedral. More in little wooden non-conformist churches.

EGERTON. This is bad for England. It turns religious worship into a hobby. Now, you are devout, sir —

GEORGE II. *(Proudly)* I am Defender of the Faith!

EGERTON. And we rejoice in your title.

GEORGE II. Come, Bishop, what do you wish me to do? Ban bees or little wooden churches?

EGERTON. We wish you to undertake an action which will rein in the moral lassitude of the nation.

GEORGE II. Bishop, the evening speeds along … If you would be so kind?

EGERTON. I need just another few moments of your time, your Majesty, if you will allow it.

GEORGE II. Do you not worry that I will not appoint you Archbishop if you weary me?

EGERTON. Your Majesty! Such thoughts never enter my mind.

GEORGE II. You are the nobility's choice for Archbishop of York, so they must enter your mind a little.

EGERTON. I feel I really must protest, sir. Ambition ill becomes the clergy.

GEORGE II. You are an exhausting man, Bishop. I need to sleep you off. Whatever it is you wanted, come see me in the morning.

EGERTON. It's about Handel, sir.

GEORGE II. Then, absolutely, it can wait 'til morning. Good night, Bishop. Have unambitious dreams.


### Scene Five
*Private room at Gopsal, Leicestershire*
*Mary Pendarves's Salon, Brook Street*
*Handel's Salon, Brook Street*
*Later that night*

*(JENNENS appears with his manuscript package and a letter.)*

JENNENS. My dear Handel. A quick addendum before I post. I am advised by other subscribers that your latest opera failed. Even the spurious royal family abandoned it. No matter: the Hanovers are a pack of usurping Huns. Not a branch of the True Line, as you know. But courage, my dear fellow. Never mind if your secular music is rubbish. It's your sacred music I want. Jennens.

*(He disappears. In her salon, MARY is serving tea to SUSANNAH, who tries her hand at light, ingratiating conversation.)*

MARY. There now, Miss Archer, this infusion will restore our nerves. Are you settled into your rooms?

SUSANNAH. Thank you, Mrs. Pendarves, they're lovely. You're very kind to let me stay.

MARY. Do call me Mary, as we have now endured a most unpleasant experience together. What shall I call you?

SUSANNAH. Please call me Maria.

MARY. What, Mary and Maria? Isn't *that* a thing?

SUSANNAH. He was frightening. I did not think he could be so angry!

MARY. Handel? Yes. Alas. Do you like my tea?

SUSANNAH. Do I detect a hint of something in it to do me good?

MARY. Just the smallest drop of vermouth. And now, dear Maria, I'm sure your life has been frightfully interesting and I've let you tell nothing of it.

SUSANNAH. *(Lightly)* Oh, no. Crowded with tedium, I assure you.

MARY. Nonsense. Do tell all.

SUSANNAH. You say Mr. Handel lives just down the street?

MARY. Yes, just down the way you're looking. That's his house. Now then, who are your young men? For someone as pretty as you must have trunkloads.

SUSANNAH. None, I fear. He seemed so desperately sad tonight.

MARY. Yes, poor man. But that has been his career, you see. Astonishing successes. Prodigious failures. But lately, alas, more of the second. *(Elsewhere HANDEL appears. He is depressed, disheveled, drinking port. He looks at some music manuscript pages.)* I came to his music when I was a girl of 13, the year he first came to London. He brought with him *Rinaldo,* his new Italian opera. *(Music from the opera drifts in as she remembers it: Lascia ch'io pianga.)* We had never heard such music. It told us every emotion of every character; nay, Maria, more: it carried us into their hearts, as though we lived their tragedies. No musician had done that before, not even dear Purcell.

*(HANDEL suddenly wads up manuscript papers in both hands.)*

SUSANNAH. You have great feeling for him.

MARY. I wedded the sainted Mr. Pendarves and may one day marry again if another worthy squire pops up, but my perpetual ravishment has been at the hands of the Master. *(HANDEL staggers off.)* I speak musically, of course.

SUSANNAH. Of course. Does he ... does he treat his singers ill? I have heard that.

MARY. Oh yes, he is a terror, a bear, to singers!

SUSANNAH. I am sorry to hear it.

MARY. It's his curse, you see.

SUSANNAH. His ill temper?

MARY. His ill singers.

SUSANNAH. But the greatest singers in Europe have sung his operas!

MARY. Oh, how shall one explain? It's deucedly hard — 'specially to one unfamiliar with the trade —

SUSANNAH. I am not so entirely unfamiliar. I have a musical brother, and —— I, myself, am somewhat musical.

MARY. Do you and are you? Hmm. Suddenly I begin to suspect this is not all idle midnight chat. I must ask you, do you wish to sing for the Master and hope I will help you to an introduction?

SUSANNAH. *(She drops all pretense now.)* You have found me out.

MARY. Well, I must observe, one feels a trifle trifled with. You have been rather cunning, have you not, seeming to be my friend?

SUSANNAH. I'm ... sorry.

MARY. Oh, I do sympathize. *(Just barely disclosing her own private dream.)* I know I should wish nothing better than to sing for the Master. Wouldn't that be a thing?

SUSANNAH. Well, then ...

MARY. No. I'm sorry. I cannot assist you. Alas, a young woman, no matter how appealing, who — and it desolates one to say it — has no reputation as a singer — you see? One cannot presume upon the Master.

SUSANNAH. No reputation?

MARY. I am frightfully sorry, but the name of Maria Archer is unknown to me as a professional singer.

SUSANNAH. I see.

MARY. And you must believe me; I would know this.

SUSANNAH. Of course. Then, may I sing for you, Mary?

MARY. What, now?

SUSANNAH. So that you may judge my gifts?

MARY. I would prefer that you would not, Maria.

SUSANNAH. Because I am unknown to you as a singer.

MARY. Oh, this is agonizing.

SUSANNAH. Please sit down, Mary.

MARY. Sit down? Why?

SUSANNAH. You said you wished to know more about me? Do you still?

MARY. Well. Now, I scarcely know.

SUSANNAH. If you are unable to remain my friend after what I tell you, I shall leave without a word.

MARY. One hardly knows what to say.

SUSANNAH. You need say nothing. Your silence will answer me.

MARY. Well, then. Go on.

SUSANNAH. Oh, Mary. I'm Susannah. Susannah Maria Cibber. *(There is, indeed, a silence. Then:)* I shall go and collect my things.

*(She leaves. MARY sits, stunned.)*

MARY. *(Quietly)* Good … heavens.

*(Crossfade to HANDEL, who cries out.)*

SMITH. *(Waking)* Crikey!

HANDEL. Smith! Where are you, Smith?

*(SMITH appears with a candle. MARY leaves. HANDEL sits up in the chair in which he has been dozing.)*

SMITH. Here, Handel.

HANDEL. You are here?

SMITH. I've been with you all dashed night.

HANDEL. I dreamed they were all gone. The King. Everyone in the town. Just only I was left, playing the organ at some theatre and no one listening! Why do they dislike my opera so?

SMITH. Never mind. They've liked others. They'll like the next one.

HANDEL. There will be no next one.

SMITH. Make no decisions in the darkest part of the night. That's what my old auntie used to say. Wait to hear what the King has to say tomorrow.

HANDEL. Ah, true. I have my appointment.

*(SMITH helps HANDEL out of his chair and towards his room.)*

SMITH. Just so. Try to sleep now, Handel.

HANDEL. Smith, your auntie with the good advice?

SMITH. Yes?

HANDEL. She never wrote an opera.

*(Back to MARY and SUSANNAH. MARY firmly pulls SUSANNAH, holding her bag and again cloaked for travel, back into the room.)*

MARY. This is too bad of you, Mrs. Cibber! You must stop trying to leave!

SUSANNAH. You can have no wish for me to stay!

MARY. It is the middle of the night! It isn't safe!

SUSANNAH. Why should I care if it's safe? *(As they struggle, SUSANNAH's straight-razor comes out of the pocket of her cloak and clatters to the floor. Both women stare at it for a moment.)* I use it for … sewing.

MARY. *(Picking up the razor.)* I believe you had better sit down, my dear. *(Suddenly weak, SUSANNAH sits.)* Is it as bad as that?

SUSANNAH. No one listens to me, you see. I haven't been a human being for a long time now. The newspapers have turned me into a … a dirty joke.

MARY. No one is that.

SUSANNAH. I saw the look on your face.

MARY. That was just …

SUSANNAH. What?

MARY. Surprise. Shock.

SUSANNAH. It was disgust.

MARY. Yes. I'm frightfully sorry.

SUSANNAH. *(Getting up.)* May I go now, please?

MARY. You say no one will listen to you. I will. I would like to. Please stay.

SUSANNAH. Why?

MARY. *(Holds up razor again.)* Well, to be frightfully candid, this for one reason. And because knowing you only half a night, I know you are not what the newspapers made you out. Will you talk to me?

*(SUSANNAH makes her decision: she will stay and talk. She puts down her bag and cloak.)*

SUSANNAH. Do you remember what the newspapers said, Mary?

MARY. Well. Let me see. They informed us that you are, or were, a singing actress and that some years ago you married Theophilus Cibber, manager of Drury Lane Theatre.

SUSANNAH. I hated him. Odious, leering man.

MARY. But then, why did you —

SUSANNAH. My father and brother told me to. He held the key to their theatrical futures.

MARY. So?

SUSANNAH. They insisted.

MARY. That is no reason!

SUSANNAH. *(Sharply)* Mary. Look around you. This beautiful, beautiful room. Have you ever known — for a day — what it is like to be poor? *(Standing and gathering her things to leave.)* Forgive me. Your kindness did not deserve that.

*(She starts to go.)*

MARY. Susannah! One is bound to say, dear child, you are something of a flibbertigibbet. Up, down, in, out. May we please continue? *(SUSANNAH sits.)* Now then. The newspapers further informed us that though your husband provided handsomely for you, you left him to contract an affair with a wealthy country gentleman —

SUSANNAH. William. Sloper.

MARY. To whom you bore a child.

SUSANNAH. That's Molly. She's with William at West Woodhay.

MARY. And you are not?

SUSANNAH. It has been determined that I should not associate with her at present.

MARY. By whom?

SUSANNAH. By William. And his family.

MARY. But surely, you have a mother's right —

SUSANNAH. Who I am is not good for Molly. Until I re-establish myself. Theophilus never provided handsomely for me. That was the biggest lie of all.

MARY. He did not?

SUSANNAH. He stole from me, all my income, everything. One night at the theatre he took every piece of jewelry I had and stripped me of every costume — including the one I was wearing. The newspapers did not write that.

MARY. No.

SUSANNAH. All to pay his horrific debts from gambling and … I may never fully recover my health. You see, Mary, my husband gave me just one present in his life. And he gave it to me in the dark.

MARY. Oh, oh dear.

SUSANNAH. Creditors still hounded us. Then Theophilus hit on a scheme. Two schemes, really. The first was to make more money from me by taking Kitty Clive's roles and making me play them. And the second …

MARY. Yes? Go on.

SUSANNAH. He came to know William, who admired my acting. And he thought, well, why not bring the two of them together? Sloper is rich. He will be well satisfied and my wife none the worse off. And my debts will be paid.

MARY. But that is —

SUSANNAH. Yes, it is. Theophilus insisted William come stay with us. And one night he kissed me on the forehead, spoke to me of duty, and pushed me across the threshold into his room.

MARY. And you could not resist him?

SUSANNAH. William was ... kind. I was unused to that. What we never knew — until the trial, of course — was that Theophilus had put a servant of his behind the wall of the bedroom. He cut eyeholes in the wainscoting and saw — everything.

MARY. Yes, you need say no more.

SUSANNAH. My husband thought he could get a large settlement, get rid of all his debts at one blow.

MARY. I know all about the trial. Everyone does.

*(But now SUSANNAH is unable to stop. Growing hysteria until the end of the scene as she relives the trial.)*

SUSANNAH. "Trial of a Cause for Criminal Conversation, between Theophilus Cibber, Plaintiff, and William Sloper, Esquire, Defendant."

MARY. Yes, that's quite enough.

SUSANNAH. Let all the town hear it! "Members of the jury, the charge is assaulting, ravishing, and carnally knowing Susannah Maria Cibber!"

MARY. Please. I do not wish to hear any more.

SUSANNAH. "Mr. Hayes. What did you see through the wainscoting?"

MARY. Susannah!

SUSANNAH. "Well your worship, meaning no offense, but I saw between five and six in the evening, he let down the turn-up bed softly. She laid herself upon it, upon her back, and pulled up her clothes —"

MARY. Stop! I demand that you stop!

SUSANNAH. "Her body was bare. He unbuttoned his clothes, let down his breeches —"

*(Suddenly and desperately, to get her to stop, MARY embraces SUSANNAH as one would a hysterical child.)*

MARY. Stop, Susannah!

SUSANNAH. *(Spent now.)* " — and lay down. Upon her."

MARY. Shh. Shh. Be quiet now.

SUSANNAH. And someone wrote a book of it all.

MARY. I know, I know. My poor child.

SUSANNAH. And filled it with awful pictures. And it's everywhere.

MARY. Don't.

SUSANNAH. And. They won't let me near my Molly.

### Scene Six
*The Salon of Handel's House, Brook Street*
*The next morning*

*(SMITH enters as the two women leave, his arms full. In a very orderly manner, he lays the table with Handel's breakfast and his own, several sheets of manuscript paper and writing equipment, and the morning post. This last includes Jennens's wrapped manuscript, another letter, and three newspapers. He looks it over, is satisfied, calls offstage.)*

SMITH. Handel!

HANDEL. *(Off)* In a moment.

SMITH. The post is in.

HANDEL. *(Off)* Anything of interest?

SMITH. *(Looking through the mail.)* Newspapers, letters from Walsh. That should have come to my house. *(He pockets it.)* Package from Leicestershire, letter from — crikey — from Dublin, Ireland.

HANDEL. *(Off)* As I thought. Nothing of interest.

SMITH. Look, Handel, are you coming? Your man's made an excellent breakfast, and it's —

HANDEL. *(Off)* Don't fret, I like it cold.

SMITH. *(To himself.)* Well, I don't.

*(He settles himself and begins eating. He picks up a newspaper and scans it. Something SMITH reads in the newspaper alarms him. Almost frantically he looks around for somewhere to hide the paper. HANDEL enters, and, seeing no place else, SMITH throws the paper under the table. HANDEL, absorbed in arranging his neck-cravat, does not see this. He carries his coat*

*and wig under an arm, and this increases his struggle with the cravat.)*

HANDEL. To hell with these new neck fashions! Smith, see to my cravat, yes?

SMITH. Certainly not. I am your treasurer. I am your copyist and liaison to your publisher. I am not your valet.

HANDEL. *(Flinging down the coat and wig.)* I am in a hurry!

SMITH. Oh, very well. *(Working on the cravat.)* We have next season to plan, you know, librettists to decide upon.

HANDEL. After my appointment with His Majesty.

SMITH. Audience, we call it, remember? Not appointment. He is the King, after all. There. You have a tied cravat.

HANDEL. Bah, we are countrymen. Why should there be ceremony? Have you computed the overages?

*(SMITH presents him with the papers.)*

SMITH. They are considerable.

HANDEL. *(He pockets the papers, begins eating his breakfast.)* I knew it would be so.

SMITH. Do you not wish to examine the losses?

*(HANDEL looks around, picks up a sheet of composition paper and tucks a corner into his cravat, using it as a bib.)*

HANDEL. The King will examine them, or one of his people. I wish only to collect the money. Ach, I have again spoiled my cravat! Will you be so kind … ?

SMITH. After your breakfast. Listen, I must tell you. We still owe from the Covent Garden season of '37 —

HANDEL. Yes, yes, I know this.

SMITH. And Signora Cuzzoni's husband is still after us for money.

HANDEL. Wicked woman! Her voice was like a donkey's!

SMITH. Her voice was exquisite. Her person was somewhat like a donkey. We have covered the losses from the last two seasons from your own accounts. If we are forced to do so again —

HANDEL. We will not, I say! This is why I go to the King! He will repair our fortunes, yes?, as he has done before.

SMITH. At times he has. At times he has not. What I am trying to say is that if this time he does not —

HANDEL. I know what you are saying! There is no need to say more!

SMITH. Yes, Handel, there is! The amount you owe approaches the staggering —

*(HANDEL rises in a passion, tearing the composition paper from his chin.)*

HANDEL. *Gott im himmel!* Will you be silent, sir? I will not hear the amount! Is this clear to you finally? The King values me! He will pay!

*(For a moment, the two look as though they might actually come to blows, leaning across the table at each other. It is SMITH who relents.)*

SMITH. Yes, I'm sure. Don't be angry.

HANDEL. Don't make me angry.

SMITH. Sorry.

HANDEL. *(It takes a moment for them to simmer down. HANDEL picks up a newspaper.)* Ah, the always edifying *London Daily Advertiser. (He pages to a familiar spot, reads.)* "At His Majesty's Theatre, Drury Lane, the initial performance of *Othello* was greeted with generous applause for Mr. Quin, as the Moor, and amusement for Mrs. Kitty Clive who, as Desdemona, managed to make of her death a comic triumph." Well, well, business as usual at Drury Lane, yes? *(Looks around the table.)* And where is the *Spectator?*

SMITH. *(Quickly picking up and tearing open the letter from Dublin to distract HANDEL from his search.)* Here is your letter from Ireland, Handel.

HANDEL. Well?

SMITH. Upon my word ...

*(Reading)*

HANDEL. What is it? Let me see. *(SMITH hands him the letter. He reads.)* "We know well the excellence of your compositions … Do us the honor of accepting an invitation to perform a season in Dublin."

SMITH. Now there's a thought. The town would miss you, and you would shine all the brighter when you return.

HANDEL. *(Crumpling letter and tossing it on the floor. SMITH discreetly picks it up.)* What is the package?

SMITH. *(Opening the package.)* It's from Mr. Jennens. Oh, it's his *Il Moderato* poem. And a letter. *(Scanning and pocketing it without showing it to the uninterested HANDEL.)* Hmm. His usual political ravings.

HANDEL. I'm sure.

SMITH. Hang on, there's another manuscript here. And another letter. *(He scans and hands the letter to HANDEL, who reads it, while he looks at the manuscript.)* "Majora canamus." What on earth does *"Majora canamus"* mean?

HANDEL. "Let us sing of greater things." It's Virgil. *(SMITH looks baffled.)* From the *Aeneid*? *(More bafflement.)* Latin? Ach, it all begins and ends at the cliffs of Dover with you English.

SMITH. I beg your pardon. Mr. Jennens is an Englishman.

HANDEL. *(He refers to the letter.)* He means me to make this into an oratorio, like his *Saul*. *(Tosses the letter away.)* Hmph.

SMITH. Do you not even wish to look at his manuscript?

HANDEL. I am as sick of religion put to music as I am of opera. *(He spies the Spectator, stoops down to reach for it.)* Ah, there is the *Spectator*, trying to hide from me.

*(He retrieves it, looks sharply at SMITH.)*

SMITH. So it is.

*(HANDEL pages through the newspaper until he comes to something that catches his interest. He reads with increasing agitation.)*

HANDEL. *(Muttering as he reads.)* What is this? No … no … Listen to this! "Handel's outburst last night may be the final disgust which causes the town to break with him entirely. How long is the public to suffer railing at his hands for merely having the good sense to stay away from his insipid operas?"

SMITH. Now, Handel, it is just the *Spectator,* a known enemy.

HANDEL. "His comparison of London to a slops bucket so far exceeds decorum and sense that one wonders if he is quite sane." I never said London was a slops bucket!

SMITH. No, you didn't, quite.

HANDEL. You told me the theatre was empty by then!

SMITH. Apparently, not entirely.

HANDEL. "He forswore opera last night; let him keep to his word, and the town will be pleased."

*(Puts the paper down, stunned.)*

SMITH. You know you must ignore it. *(In answer, HANDEL nods, walks despondently round to the back of the table, sits. After a moment:)* Your operas have frequently been packed with people almost mad to see them.

HANDEL. In former days.

SMITH. The queen was your loyal patron.

HANDEL. Yes. I would to God she was still alive.

SMITH. You are the greatest organist in Europe. You —

HANDEL. Yes, yes, Smith, enough.

SMITH. Quite enough, I agree, of heeding the jealous ravings of one lone crank *(Taking the paper from HANDEL'S numb hands.)* who hasn't even the courage to sign his name. Now, we must select a theatre for your next opera.

HANDEL. I take my oath before God and you. I will never write another opera. The town has turned against them. And, finally so have I.

SMITH. Well, what then? Instrumental music? Walsh would love that. Your opus 6 sold very well.

HANDEL. Ah, yes! How about, to go with the music for the coronation and the music for the water, music for a dog show? *(KITTY CLIVE enters, unseen by the two men.)* The public will adore it; they will hardly need even to pay attention. La la la, woof woof woof.

    KITTY. Mr. Handel?

*(SMITH and HANDEL are both surprised.)*

    SMITH. Who are you?

    HANDEL. How did you get in here?

    KITTY. Your man let me in.

    HANDEL. Le Blond presumes a great deal just because he can cook! Well, now you can go. I have an appointment with the King!

*(Starts to go.)*

    KITTY. Wait! I am a singer!

    HANDEL. Of course you are. What a pity! *(Gets to the door.)* Excuse me.

    KITTY. *(To SMITH.)* Why doesn't the man listen? *(To both.)* I am Mrs. Catherine Clive of His Majesty's Theatre, Drury Lane.

*(This stops HANDEL.)*

    SMITH. Kitty Clive? But Mrs. Pendarves was to have told you not to come this morning.

    KITTY. I know no one of that name.

    SMITH. Yes, well you'll have to come back some other time, Mrs. Clive. I'm sorry.

    HANDEL. *(He turns around, delighted.)* Desdemona?

    KITTY. I beg your pardon?

    HANDEL. You are Desdemona?

    KITTY. That is the role I currently have the honor to portray, yes.

    HANDEL. Well, well, Mrs. Clive of Drury Lane.

    KITTY. A name not unknown to you, sir, I dare say.

    HANDEL. I dare say, too. Forgive me, after many years, I am still somewhat the foreigner in your country. I do not know your local playwrights as I should. Desdemona. Is this a comic role?

KITTY. Certainly not. It is one of the Bard's most thrillingly tragical roles.

HANDEL. Could you, perhaps, do a little of it for us?

KITTY. Well …

SMITH. Handel, the woman came to sing.

HANDEL. No doubt, yes. But a singer of operas must have dramatic qualities. I would like to see some Desdemona.

KITTY. You're making sport of me! Don't think I don't see that!

HANDEL. Madam, I never make sport; I am German! You wish to make an impression upon me, yes?, to appear in a Handel opera. This is why you are here?

KITTY. Yes. But to sing. I have an aria from your *Alcina*.

HANDEL. Perhaps later. Right now, I would simply like to evaluate your dramatic talents.

KITTY. I see. Very well. Then I shall show you the death scene, as it's quite dramatic. Desdemona dies. Tragically.

HANDEL. Don't they all?

KITTY. Violently smothered by her brute of a jealous husband.

HANDEL. Smith! You did that once to a wife, did you not?

SMITH. Oh really, let the woman get on . You'll be late.

HANDEL. Forgive me, Mrs. Clive. Go on.

KITTY. Are you sure? I really came to sing.

HANDEL. Oh, please, Mrs. Clive.

KITTY. Well, then, I'm on the bed, you see. And he comes in all murderous and wakes me up. "O, banish me, my lord, but kill me not!" Then he has a bit. Then, "Kill me tomorrow, let me live tonight." Then his bit again. "But half an hour!" Him again. "But while I say one prayer!" Him one more time, then down with the pillow on me face *(She grabs the Spectator, covers her face with it.)* so I must use all the power of me voice to be heard in the gallery. *(Covers her face and yells out, muffled.)* "Oh Lord, Lord, Lord!"

HANDEL. *(Takes a moment.)* This is the end?

KITTY. Yes. I'm dead now.

HANDEL. Fascinating. *(Starts to go again.)* Good morning.

*(He picks up his wig, plonks it on his head.)*

KITTY. But my aria! You must listen to me sing.

HANDEL. *(Examines his watch.)* Oh dear, I am in great danger of being late.

KITTY. Mr. Handel, I have taken time out of a very busy day to come here —

SMITH. With no appointment.

KITTY. — to offer you my services as a soprano. May I not sing for you?

HANDEL. No.

KITTY. You think, coming from Drury Lane, my voice is not good enough for the opera.

HANDEL. No doubt, it is too good. Like all sopranos you take great joy, I am sure, in flourishing and cutting capers with your excellent voice. Ach, I am sick of it! Now go away, please.

KITTY. I won't!

HANDEL. *(Picks up the Advertiser and flourishes it at KITTY.)* Go back to Drury Lane and play some more of your comic Desdemona.

KITTY. You! You *have* made sport of me! You — poisonous, puffed up, old hog!

HANDEL. Listen to me, Mrs. Clive. They say I once threw a castrato out a window. I make sopranos weep, like that! *(Snaps his fingers.)* Now go away before I live up to my reputation!

KITTY. *(She hurriedly makes preparations to depart.)* Oh Lord, I'll go, you can be sure of that. I curse myself for coming in the first place! Why should an actress of my parts and qualities link herself with the wreckage of your career? *(Flourishes the Spectator at HANDEL.)* Deidamia! I wouldn't blot me make-up with the score!

HANDEL. Indeed, there would not be enough pages.

KITTY. How dare you use me for your amusement! I'm Catherine Clive! Who are you? Someone no person of quality wants to know! Why, you're so unpopular now, you couldn't even get the clap!

*(KITTY throws the newspaper at HANDEL and exits.)*

SMITH. You have twenty minutes to get to the Palace.

### Scene Seven
*Private room at Gopsal, Leicestershire*
*Audience Chamber, St. James's Palace*
*The same morning*

*(JENNENS is writing another letter as HANDEL and SMITH exit.)*

JENNENS. My dear Handel. When I said your operas are rubbish, it was not meant to be discouraging. I'm certain that you can set my scripture collection to the lofty music it requires — if you overcome your natural inclination toward laziness. What I intend — *(He suddenly balls up the letter.)* Oh, never mind. I'll tell him myself. *(He grabs his overcoat and exits, calling off.)* Pack up!

*(EGERTON and the KING are in mid-conversation, appearing as JENNENS disappears.)*

GEORGE II. Yes, Bishop, but still you are unclear. What do you want from me? The morning speeds along.

EGERTON. *(He pulls out a copy of the* Spectator, *hands it to the KING.)* Have you seen this, sir? The letter I have marked. *(The KING takes the paper, reads a bit of the article.)* It's Handel. He has put the whole town against him this time. Apparently his behavior last night at some theatre was shockingly rude.

GEORGE II. *Ja,* so I am reading.

EGERTON. I know that your Majesty has been his supporter.

GEORGE II. Not since the Queen died.

EGERTON. Well, you know the Church is always supportive of art when it uplifts. But Handel's theatre music we find unwholesome. Many of the cloth think theatres little better than bawdy houses, as it is.

GEORGE II. I have attended the theatre. With my family.

EGERTON. The royal family, of course, dwells on the heights of Parnassus, where all is pure and devotional.

GEORGE II. Well, I don't know about Parnassus. We sit in the royal box. Come to the point. What has all this to do with Handel? Do you object to his latest opera? *(Consults newspaper.)* It is too late; it seems to be over.

EGERTON. Well, yes. But that is not my point.

GEORGE II. Well, what is, Bishop? Is there one?

EGERTON. It is these oratorios, sir. They corrode the soul. You must prohibit them.

GEORGE II. What, you mean like *Saul*? Wasn't *Saul* an oratorio?

EGERTON. Yes, indeed it was, your Majesty.

GEORGE II. Well, what was wrong with *Saul*? It was from the Bible! You should love it, just like a sermon on the stage.

EGERTON. That is exactly the point, your Majesty. Sermons should be left to the clergy, and they should be delivered in churches.

GEORGE II. Why?

EGERTON. Well think of it, your Majesty. Scriptures mouthed by lewd players and sung to low opera tunes. At theatres! It is blasphemous.

GEORGE II. Queen Caroline liked *Saul*.

EGERTON. Ah.

GEORGE II. And so, I did, too.

EGERTON. I see. Yes, of course. *(He must try a different strategy.)* Your Majesty. You may not be aware of who wrote *Saul*.

GEORGE II. Of course I am aware. It was Handel.

EGERTON. He wrote the music — or stole it, no doubt, as is his usual practice. But the words, sir, were written by Charles Jennens, the non-juror.

GEORGE II. What is that? Another word for bee-keeping?

EGERTON. It is what we call a man who refuses to sign the loyalty oath to the House of Hanover.

GEORGE II. I did not know this.

EGERTON. Think of what his oratorio, *Saul*, is about: the deposing of a King by an upstart from another family.

GEORGE II. David. *Ja.* That is true. I never thought of it.

EGERTON. This Jennens also wrote the libretto for Handel's *Israel in Egypt*.

GEORGE II. I do not like *Israel in Egypt*.

EGERTON. Well, no one did. But, again, think of the subject. Revolution. People rising up against a King.

GEORGE II. *(The light is dawning.)* Oh, *ja*. The children of Israel. Against poor Pharaoh.

*(HANDEL enters, bows.)*

HANDEL. *Guten morgan*, your Majesty.

GEORGE II. Ah, Handel, you have come. *(The KING rises, and they greet each other warmly, kissing on both cheeks.)* Do you know Bishop Egerton?

HANDEL. I do not. Good morning.

EGERTON. Mr. Handel.

GEORGE II. Shall we all sit and be informal? *(Indicates for HANDEL to sit.)* This is not the French court, after all. How is your health, Handel?

HANDEL. I am keeping well.

GEORGE II. No more paralyzed arm?

HANDEL. No. Thank you. Majesty, I had hoped *mit Ihnen allein zu sprechen (Speak with you alone)*.

GEORGE II. Speak alone? Oh, no, Handel, for then, you know, we would fall to talking German together, and that addles my English. We will keep Bishop Egerton with us to make sure this does not happen. If this is convenient for you, Bishop?

EGERTON. I am delighted to stay.

HANDEL. I see.

GEORGE II. *(Casually shows newspaper.)* What is this I read in the paper of you, Handel? You have been shouting at audiences.

HANDEL. Majesty, I did not see you at *Deidamia*.

GEORGE II. No.

EGERTON. His Majesty has affairs of state to attend to. He cannot always be running to amusements.

HANDEL. How do you know this, sir? Is the clergy now arranging the royal calendar?

GEORGE II. You know I have lost my taste for these things.

HANDEL. Also you did not subscribe to my new concerti, Majesty. Allow me to present you with a copy.

*(He takes a bound manuscript from a case, holds it out for the KING.)*

GEORGE II. *(He does not take it.)* Why do I need these? I have Bach's *Brandenburg Concerti. (This renders HANDEL speechless.)*

Come, Handel, give me your expenses for the season. This is why you come to me, *ja*? For money? Come, come, give them to me. *(HANDEL turns over the papers to the KING, who examines them.)* Bishop, you, perhaps, do not know how expensive operas are.

EGERTON. No, your Majesty, but I am told all the gilt and finery can be very costly.

GEORGE II. Dear me, yes. It is like keeping a harem to pay for opera year after year. But I am no sultan of Persia, *ja*?, just the poor King of England. I do have the right still to be King, Handel?

HANDEL. Of course, Majesty. What —

GEORGE II. What are you working on?

HANDEL. Now, Majesty?

GEORGE II. *Ja, ja.* Right now. You must always be working if I am to pay your debts.

EGERTON. Surely you are collaborating with some librettist on a sublime new work.

HANDEL. No.

GEORGE II. You see, Bishop. Artists are not careful with money.

HANDEL. *(Thinking desperately.)* Well. Then, yes. I'm — working on a new oratorio, Majesty. Yes. This will interest you, Bishop, I think. It is a new sacred work.

EGERTON. Indeed?

HANDEL. Yes, you know, Majesty, taken from the Bible, like *Saul,* which Queen Caroline enjoyed so.

EGERTON. What is the subject? Another Old Testament story of rebellion?

HANDEL. *Majora canamus*. The mystery of godliness.

EGERTON. What! You propose to write an opera —

HANDEL. An oratorio!

EGERTON. Call it what you will! An entertainment — about Our Lord?

HANDEL. *(Puzzled)* Yes.

EGERTON. *(Stands in horror.)* Your Majesty!

GEORGE II. *(Stands to calm him.)* You must be calm, Bishop. Archbishops are always calm. Who is writing the libretto?

HANDEL. Mr. Jennens.

EGERTON. The non-juror.
GEORGE II. I see.
HANDEL. He wrote the book for *Saul,* you remember.
GEORGE II. *Ja,* I do.

*(The KING stands, HANDEL'S accounts still in his hand. He walks a bit, considering. HANDEL and EGERTON watch, wondering what will come next. The KING hands HANDEL the debt sheet.)*

GEORGE II. I do not believe the Treasury can undertake your debts this year. *(HANDEL sits in silence. The KING suddenly becomes angry.)* Why are you sitting, Handel? I, the King, am standing! One stands in the presence of one's betters!

*(HANDEL stands despondently as the KING sweeps from the room, followed by the BISHOP. Now HANDEL becomes the still point around which the scene shifts. SMITH comes on and we are once again in HANDEL'S salon.)*

### Scene Eight
*The Salon of Handel's House, Brook Street*
*Later the same day*

*(HANDEL pulls off his wig sadly.)*

SMITH. Well, no matter. It's not as if your credit isn't good in town. Any number of establishments will lend you money against next season.
HANDEL. I lied.
SMITH. About what?
HANDEL. I told his Majesty I was setting Mr. Jennens's libretto. He said I must always be working.
SMITH. Well, good. Set it then. Mr. Jennens is a fine librettist.
HANDEL. I'm going home.
SMITH. This is your house. You *are* home.
HANDEL. No. I mean home. Back to Germany.
SMITH. You're a British subject now.

HANDEL. I even changed my name from Friederic to Frederick to match the Prince of Wales. But still I am a foreigner.

SMITH. You're no more a foreigner than the King of England!

*(MARY enters tentatively.)*

MARY. Knock, knock.

HANDEL. My arm hurts. Look, I can hardly move it. I want to go home.

MARY. One doesn't like to intrude. Le Blond said to come straight up.

SMITH. Ah, Ms. Pendarves, do come in, please. Look, Handel, it's Mrs. Pendarces.

MARY. *(Low voice.)* Is the Master out of sorts?

SMITH. *(Low voice.)* Perhaps you can cheer him.

MARY. *(Low voice.)* I was unable to apprehend the Clive woman last night.

SMITH. *(Low voice.)* She was here this morning.

MARY. *(Low voice.)* Oh dear. *(Going to HANDEL.)* Good afternoon, Herr Handel, how are you? One is frightfully sorry for being the cause of that Clive creature troubling you.

HANDEL. *(Meaning, it's alright.)* No, no.

MARY. Your *Deidamia.* It was exquisite! I had to come tell you. Each note was breathed upon by the muses. One was absolutely ravished!

HANDEL. It was not so good as *Imeneo.*

MARY. Yes it was! Both operas were celestial spheres humming in tune with the divine!

SMITH. There you are, Handel! Celestial spheres! And Mrs. Pendarves knows her music.

HANDEL. The town did not agree.

MARY. I have recently discovered a thing or two about the town. It seems to believe what the newspapers tell it. This makes it, one is sorry to say, an ass.

SMITH. Dashed well said!

MARY. All *Deidamia* wanted was a soprano worthy of it.

HANDEL. Do you think so?

MARY. And I have discovered a solution to that problem. I have found the Master a new singer!

HANDEL. Ach!

MARY. This young woman has a voice like the rustle of doves' wings!

SMITH. Oh, no, Mrs. Pendarves, it's really most kind of you, but —

MARY. Now, you mustn't say no! You mustn't! Herr Handel, what do you say? *(She gives him no time to form a coherent reply.)* Excellent! I shan't be a moment, the young woman is right outside!

*(She disappears.)*

HANDEL. No! Mrs. Pendarves! *(But she is gone.)* Two sopranos in one day.

*(MARY comes back in, leading SUSANNAH by the hand.)*

MARY. There now. She is pretty as two pictures, is she not? And wait until you hear her sing! You shall melt. I did. Herr Handel, Mr. Smith, this is Mrs. Susannah Cibber. Dear Susannah, these are Mr. John Christopher Smith and the Master.

SMITH. *(Knows the name.)* My word! Mrs. Cibber?

SUSANNAH. How do you do?

SMITH. My word.

MARY. He does well, don't you, Mr. Smith?

SMITH. Yes. It is a pleasure to actually meet you, ma'am. In the flesh. No, that's badly said; I mean, I have seen your picture ... No! Oh, dear ...

SUSANNAH. It's quite alright, Mr. Smith.

SMITH. You servant, madam.

*(HANDEL gets up and peers at her.)*

HANDEL. I am not seeing more sopranos today. Good day, young lady.

SUSANNAH. I thought I might sing for you, sir.

HANDEL. No! She must go, Mrs. Pendarves!

MARY. Herr Handel! You must stop this — hastiness. It is too bad.

HANDEL. Wait. Wait a moment. Cibber? I am remembering now — you ran off and had consummation with the rich country man, and there was a most diverting adultery trial.

MARY. Oh, Herr Handel!

HANDEL. And then someone wrote a dirty book about it all. Since then, you have been hiding out, yes?

MARY. Herr Handel! You do not know — indeed, perhaps your sex can never know — what this poor woman has suffered.

HANDEL. Smith, what did I say? Do I give offense?

SMITH. Frequently.

HANDEL. Ach! I apologize, Mrs. Cibber. This has been a difficult day for me.

SUSANNAH. I'm sorry. Still, I would so like to sing for you.

MARY. And one is bound to say you'll profit by it.

SMITH. Perhaps this is not really the time.

HANDEL. No, no, Smith, I do not wish to offend Mrs. Pendarves and her sex. Go on, Mrs. Cibber. Yes. Please do sing. Do you wish accompaniment?

SUSANNAH. No. I thought, just something simple.

HANDEL. Begin when you will.

*(With no more ceremony than that, she sings "The Coventry Carol". It was said of SUSANNAH CIBBER that she sang with simple sweetness and feeling, qualities that appealed to HANDEL.)*

SUSANNAH. *(The Coventry Carol)*
Lully, lulla, thou little tiny child,
By by, lully lullay

Herod the king, in his raging
Chargèd he hath this day
His men of might, in his own sight,
All young children to slay.

Then woe is me, poor child, for thee!
And ever mourn and sigh,
For thy parting neither say nor sing
By by, lully lullay.

HANDEL. *(Moved by the singing.)* Amen.

MARY. There now. What did I tell you?

SMITH. You have a beautiful voice, Mrs. Cibber.

HANDEL. No curlicues. Just the notes. This is the voice of an angel.

SUSANNAH. Thank you.

HANDEL. *(Sighs)* Which makes it all the more sad. I must tell you, if there was going to be a next season, you would sing in it. But there will not be.

MARY. What! This is not conceivable!

HANDEL. Oh yes, it is even a fact. Dear Mrs. Cibber, this town has given us both the boot, yes?

MARY. But what do you intend to do?

HANDEL. I will go home to Germany, I think. Perhaps I will go to Leipzig to see Bach. Maybe he will let me turn his pages while he plays the organ.

*(JENNENS enters, still in his coat. He has just traveled down from Gopsal.)*

JENNENS. There you are, Handel!

*(HANDEL looks wearily around to see him.)*

HANDEL. Oh no.

JENNENS. Le Blond said to come up.

*(Music begins immediately: "Her Body is Buried in Peace" from Funeral Anthem for Queen Caroline.)*

### Scene Nine
*The Henry VII Chapel, Westminster Abbey*
*August, 1741*

*(Light, from a stained-glass window, discovers the KING, flowers in hand, standing alone, grief-stricken. He is before the tomb of his wife, which is marked only by a pavement in the floor. He places the flowers on the appropriate spot. EGERTON enters behind. Music fades.)*

EGERTON. "For as in Adam all die, even so in Christ shall all be made alive."

*(He crosses himself.)*

GEORGE II. Amen.

*(Crosses himself.)*

EGERTON. A gentle harmony arose in England while this Royal Lady lived.

GEORGE II. *Ja.* But I was thinking of her funeral. Do you remember, Bishop?

EGERTON. Freezing cold. There was ice in the nave. But, somehow, here in this chapel, it was warm.

GEORGE II. Two and a half years ago. But for me, just last night. When the yeomen of the guard brought her casket in, everyone was in tears, but not me. I could not believe it, you see. I still cannot believe it. My father had his mistresses, damn him; and no doubt so does my worthless son. I had Caroline.

EGERTON. The nation still feels your loss.

GEORGE II. And then, the music began. Handel's music. Caroline loved his music. He wrote duets for her when she was a girl in Hanover. This time he wrote for her a funeral anthem.

EGERTON. Yes.

GEORGE II. It was ... the most beautiful music ever written. Very German, you know. And, for me, it was as if angels came down when the choir sang. I saw them. They took my Caroline by the hand

and flew with her, up, through the vault, up away to heaven. *(Breaking down a little.)* Oh, Caroline. Can you not come down for me? I am so lonely here now. Ach! I am sorry, Bishop.

EGERTON. No, no, your Majesty, you must not apologize.

GEORGE II. You see, there are many times now when I wish simply to go home to her.

EGERTON. I am truly sorry, your Majesty.

GEORGE II. *Ja.* But Handel. Do you know what he did with the Queen's funeral music? He ate it all back up and spat it out a year later into an oratorio.

EGERTON. Ah. *Israel in Egypt.*

GEORGE II. The music which carried her up into heaven — he stole it from her.

EGERTON. Abominable. It is what I have been trying to say, sir. How could he take the Queen's sacred music and give it to a lewd theatre crowd?

GEORGE II. *(Unheeding)* I did not attend Israel in Egypt.

EGERTON. Indeed, how could you?

GEORGE II. I have not heard his music since. I used to enjoy it, but now …

EGERTON. Now you find it blasphemous, sir.

GEORGE II. I find it unimportant. It does not come to my heart any more. And now, Bishop, there is the Privy Council and Walpole.

EGERTON. If you wish to commune privately, your Majesty, I can withdraw.

GEORGE II. Have you not been listening? I cannot commune with the Queen. She is not here. I thought you would know this.

*(The KING looks once more to the pavement, crosses himself again, and leaves. EGERTON remains. KITTY CLIVE, who has been listening, out of sight, approaches him.)*

KITTY. Who'd've thought he was so sentimental? He's an old dear, really, isn't he?

EGERTON. Have you been eavesdropping, madam?

KITTY. He's had mistresses, too, I expect. Still …

EGERTON. Still, he may mourn his wife. You have the advantage of me, madam.

KITTY. Do I? Well, I know you. You're the renowned Henry Egerton, the most passionate divine in all the town, what makes hearts beat faster as we gaze up into heaven.

*(She touches him. It doesn't work.)*

EGERTON. Madam.

*(She withdraws her hand.)*

KITTY. And I'm Catherine Clive. That's a name you've heard, I expect. You'll have seen my Polly from *The Beggar's Opera.*
EGERTON. I don't frequent theatres.
KITTY. Well, I'm frequenting this church at the moment. Aren't you the tiniest bit curious to know why?
EGERTON. I'm bound as a Christian to say, not particularly.
KITTY. It's something I heard Mr. Quin say at the theatre. He heard it directly from Mr. Charles Macklin, who, as you must know, moves in Palace circles, as they say.
EGERTON. Do they? Your servant, madam. Enjoy the monuments.

*(He starts to go.)*

KITTY. Mr. Macklin says that you don't care much for German pig these days.
EGERTON. *(This stops him.)* German pig, madam?
KITTY. Oh, you know the sort I mean. The kind that gets up on its hind legs every now and again and composes an opera. Or an oratorio. Well, perhaps Mr. Macklin was misinformed. Good day.
EGERTON. Wait! How do you know these things? Are you an opera singer?
KITTY. Opera?! Lord, no! Oh, I once sang — that sort of music — for Handel, as you would know if you followed the careers of great artists. But since I have seen the light I will no longer fill my throat with his nauseous songs.
EGERTON. I see, I see.

KITTY. Of course, it is his oratorios which are my particular aversion.

EGERTON. Really?

KITTY. They so offend the higher sensibilities. Don't they?

EGERTON. Yes! I've been trying to make that very point to his Majesty!

KITTY. They cause me acute spiritual distress. *(Touches her heart.)* It hurts me here.

EGERTON. When did this change of heart occur, Mrs. Clive?

KITTY. Why, surely you must guess! It was when I heard you preach on the subject at St. Paul's. What a transforming sermon it was! You are quite powerful, Bishop.

EGERTON. Am I?

KITTY. Yes. Oh, oh, yes. And I'm just wondering. Is there anything I can do to help?

### *Scene Ten*

*The Salon of Handel's House, Brook Street*
*Audience Chamber, St. James's Palace*
*The Salon of Mary Pendarves's House, Brook Street*
*August 22*

*(As KITTY and EGERTON exit, JENNENS and SMITH carry in and set down a light, wooden frame and a chair. Meanwhile, HANDEL is absorbed in composing at his table and does not notice them. They leave and come back in with a harpsichord, which they set carefully on the frame.)*

SMITH. Thank you, Mr. Jennens.

JENNENS. Not at all.

SMITH. There you are, Handel. It's the new instrument. Mr. Jennens arranged for it to be brought straight over.

HANDEL. *(Not really looking up.)* Yes, yes.

JENNENS. *(At the harpsichord.)* Come look. It's a Rucker's.

*(JENNENS plunks a few keys.)*

HANDEL. I know what you are thinking, Mr. Jennens: I will come to that harpsichord, and sit down and play, yes?

JENNENS. *(Plays a little.)* My word. *(A little more.)* This is quite good, really.

HANDEL. And, having played a note or two, suddenly I will be enraptured.

JENNENS. I must get one up at Gopsal.

HANDEL. "Oh my!" I will say. "I feel the inspiration coming all over me like St. Elmo's fire! I must immediately begin setting Mr. Jennens's oratorio!" In every month since your arrival you have thought up some new way to get me to do it.

JENNENS. Never mind. *(About the harpsichord.)* This will look very handsome in my music room.

*(HANDEL gets up quickly, suddenly finding that he wants to play the new instrument.)*

HANDEL. Alright! To please you. *(He goes over and plays a note or two. Meanwhile, SMITH looks at the manuscript HANDEL has been writing.)* Bah! Out of tune.

*(He takes out a tuning key from its place in the harpsichord, begins to tighten a string.)*

SMITH. Handel! You've been writing! Can this be published? Walsh will want to know. I want to know!

HANDEL. It's nothing — just some little Italian duets.

SMITH. *(Sets down the manuscript with disgust.)* You haven't written these for, what, thirty years? They're out of date. No one will publish these.

HANDEL. Who cares?

JENNENS. *(Taking out Messiah manuscript.)* Saul was a success, you know. The Haymarket was packed for twelve nights. I flatter myself that my libretto was in some measure responsible.

HANDEL. Yes, yes. I tell you again. Saul was good.

JENNENS. *(Putting his manuscript on the harpsichord in front of HANDEL.)* This is better.

HANDEL. Wait! Stop! I do not wish to hear! I have said! Take your libretto to Porpora!

SMITH. Oh, really, Handel! Will you hear the man out for once! You're fortunate to have any collaborator these days, let alone one of Mr. Jennens's quality.

HANDEL. Oh, fortunate, am I?

SMITH. Yes! Indeed you are!

HANDEL. I am done with composing!

SMITH. Then what are you doing moping around London all these months? I thought you were going back to Germany.

HANDEL. When my health permits it.

SMITH. Your health is better than mine! *(Picks up Italian duets manuscript.)* And why are you scribbling these things? Well?

HANDEL. *(Bangs the harpsichord keys.)* Damn you, Smith, I must write something! I cannot stop myself, God help me.

*(He sits miserably on the stool.)*

SMITH. Then, listen to what Mr. Jennens has to say about his libretto. Please.

HANDEL. If I do, then we will be done? Yes? If I hear you out for once, as Smith says?

JENNENS. Yes, if you listen attentively.

SMITH. You will, won't you? And not interrupt?

HANDEL. I shall be all sharply pricked ears.

SMITH. And no mouth, one hopes.

HANDEL. Alright! Go on, Mr. Jennens. *(Suddenly impatient to get it over with.)* Go on, go on, go on!

JENNENS. Very well. Well. I have said that *Messiah* takes the form of an opera. But it has no story.

HANDEL. No story!

SMITH. Handel!

HANDEL. Sorry. *(Sarcastically)* Hmm. No story. How interesting and novel. Please continue.

JENNENS. There are no named characters. Our Lord, for example, never speaks, at all. Not in his own voice. It's all scriptures, you see, which I've put together in a particular way. *(Pages through manuscript.)* Starting with prophecies of the Blesséd birth and concluding with the One Mighty and Strong enthroned in the heavens. Here, let me read you a little.

SMITH. By all means.

*(The KING comes on with some bills of appointment to the civil list. He sits at the table and signs or affixes his seal to one after another of them. He is in the audience chamber of St. James's Palace.)*

JENNENS. Everyone assembles on the stage. You, Handel, are at the harpsichord. Now. No overture. This is crucial. From out of the silence we hear the first recitative. *(He reads from the manuscript, as the KING looks up from his work, gazes sadly out.)* "Comfort ye, comfort ye, my people." It's from Isaiah.

*(The KING resumes his task. SUSANNAH comes on, dressed for travel and with luggage. She is in Mary Pendarves's salon.)*

HANDEL. Are you going to read the whole thing, Mr. Jennens?
JENNENS. *(He pages through the manuscript as SUSANNAH sits on her luggage.)* Ah, here's a part you'll like. More Isaiah, but it's something like a story. *(Music under.)* "Behold a Virgin shall conceive, and bear a Son, and shall call his name Emmanuel, God with us." *(HANDEL looks over and sees SUSANNAH. He is transfixed. Perhaps he even stands.)* This is where we first hear tidings of the Blesséd Virgin."
HANDEL. Yes.

*(JENNENS, puzzled, hesitates. He looks to SMITH.)*

SMITH. Read a little more.
JENNENS. Surely. Let me see. *(Pages through the manuscript.)* Oh yes. "He was despised and rejected of men. A man of sorrows and acquainted with grief."
HANDEL. *(This catches his attention.)* What? What was that?
JENNENS. It's what happened to Our Lord. Now the music for this must be sublime, celestial ... Handel?

HANDEL. May I see this manuscript, please?
JENNENS. Yes. Certainly.

*(He hands it over.)*

SMITH. Bravo, Mr. Jennens!
JENNENS. What did I do?
HANDEL. May I ask both of you please to be still for a few moments?
JENNENS. *(Baffled)* Of course.
SMITH. He'll be hearing the music, you see.
JENNENS. Oh. We could go, if that would be better.
HANDEL. You are most considerate. It would be better.
JENNENS. I leave it in your hands, then.

*(They go. As HANDEL reads, MARY comes into her salon.)*

MARY. My man has gone for a hansom to take you to the coach.
SUSANNAH. How can I repay your kindness to me?
MARY. Oh, never think of that. But where are you going? Yes, I know, Dublin, the far Hibernian shore, to act dramatic parts with Mr. Quin, but —
SUSANNAH. It is the only offer I have received. I must be grateful.
MARY. But your rehearsals don't begin for two months. What will you do in the meantime?
SUSANNAH. I don't know. But I must leave now or I feel I shall … I shall fall in on myself, the town presses on me so. *(Takes out a letter.)* Will you please see that this goes up to William at West Woodhay? *(Takes out a doll with a note pinned to it.)* And this for Molly? I should have wrapped it.
MARY. *(Taking the things and embracing her.)* Oh, you do break one's heart! God bless you, dear child. Fly straight back to me in the spring.

*(MARY leaves. HANDEL continues to read. EGERTON comes in. Without even looking up, the KING knows it is he.)*

GEORGE II. *Ja,* Bishop, what is it? I am approving the civil lists, you see? This makes me busy.

EGERTON. I … This will take only a moment, sir, if you'll allow me. *(Produces a small book.)* I don't know if you know the writings of Boethius?

GEORGE II. No.

EGERTON. One of the ancient philosophers. After my mother died, I found his words consoling.

GEORGE II. *(Looks up.) Ja?*

EGERTON. I thought — after our talk at the Abbey … well. I've brought a German translation.

GEORGE II. *(Takes the offered book.)* You are very kind. Also, I find, you are quite sincere.

EGERTON. Sir?

GEORGE II. All this about music. It is not just because you want to be Archbishop of York.

EGERTON. I find the northern climate uncongenial, your Majesty.

GEORGE II. *(Laughs briefly.) Ja.* That's why there's an opening, I think. Well, Bishop, you have good qualities.

EGERTON. Thank you, your Majesty.

GEORGE II. But you must be careful, *ja?* Good qualities are hard to overcome. Good night, Bishop.

*(EGERTON leaves. As HANDEL reads, we hear hints of music. SUSANNAH waits.)*

HANDEL. *(Reading aloud.)* "He was despised." Exactly. *(Skips ahead.)* "Thy rebuke hath broken his heart." *(Skips ahead.)* "He looked for some to have pity on him, but there was no man, neither found he any to comfort him." *(He does not need to read any more.)* Smith! *(SMITH and JENNENS enter.)* Ah, Smith, will you be so kind?

SMITH. Composition sheets! Right!

*(He leaves to get them.)*

JENNENS. You like my scripture collection, then?

HANDEL. It speaks directly to me, sir.

JENNENS. I am very gratified. And the plan I made for divisions into arias, choruses, and so on?

HANDEL. Well, some of this will change, of course —

JENNENS. Yes, a little, I suppose —

*(SMITH returns with the large sheets, which he puts down on the harpsichord.)*

SMITH. I really was afraid you would go back to Germany.

HANDEL. *(Seizes the paper, takes a quill from the table, and begins writing.)* Well, Smith. Germany. It's filled with Germans, you know. Maybe I will go to Ireland, instead, where they have such good taste.

SMITH. *(Producing the crumpled letter from Dublin.)* I thought you might.

HANDEL. Anyway, right now, I am writing! You both must leave me. Smith, lock the doors. Tell Le Blond to start cooking. Goodbye, Mr. Jennens.

JENNENS. I thought I would stay, perhaps give an impression here and there.

HANDEL. Out of the question. Goodbye.

SMITH. It *is* best to go, Mr. Jennens, really. Congratulations, sir.

JENNENS. Well, then, alright. Good luck, Handel.

HANDEL. *(Absorbed. More hints of* Messiah *music come softly in.)* Thank you, thank you, and to you. Goodbye. *(SMITH looks over at the KING, then SUSANNAH. Music cuts off abruptly.)* "He was despised." Yes.

*(He returns to writing. Blackout. The Overture to* Messiah *begins immediately. It plays through the first minutes of the intermission to its conclusion.)*

## ACT II

### Scene One

St. Paul's Cathedral
Private room at Gopsal, Leicestershire
Mary Pendarves's Salon, Brook Street
The first Sunday of January, 1743, Matins
Two separate days in January

*(During the last portion of the intermission, the music of an era-appropriate hymn or psalm setting has been heard, as though in a cathedral. It continues as the house lights go down and BISHOP EGERTON enters. He is preaching at St. Paul's. Hymn ends.)*

EGERTON. I pray that you may eschew those things which are contrary to the faith, and follow only what is agreeable to it. Through Jesus Christ, our Lord. Amen.

CONGREGATION. *(Off. Simultaneously with EGERTON.)* Amen.

EGERTON. I have been meditating on the passage from Romans, read to us in the Second Lesson. *(Reads)* "Now I beseech you, brethren, mark them which cause divisions and offenses contrary to the doctrine which ye have learned." But what should be our attitude towards persons who *do* cause offense? *(Reads)* "For they that are such serve not our Lord Jesus Christ, but their own belly." Now whenever I read the word, belly, one particular person comes to mind. Once, in the days when he served God, he regularly played this very organ. *(The massive pipes are behind and above him.)* But over the years, he has become a stranger to righteousness. Recently he concluded a musical season in Ireland, where he performed a new oratorio. Now, you know that I have spoken out against this pernicious practice of turning the Bible into entertainment. But this new musical abomination goes beyond even the blasphemies of the

53

past. I am informed that it is called *Messiah*. Yes! One of the titles of Our Lord.

*(JENNENS, at Gopsal, writing a letter.)*

JENNENS. My dear Handel. I received with pleasure here at Gopsal your account of *Messiah's* success in Dublin. But still you do not send me your orchestrations. Where is the score?

EGERTON. Picture that sacred word — Messiah — on playbills stuck up in Smock Alley and Pudding Lane to be chortled over by gin-drinking louts and infamous women! It is abominable! And yet it will happen. Covetous of lucre to serve his belly, this composer means to inflict his oratorio on the town in less than three months time.

JENNENS. Where in London do you intend to perform it? I thought perhaps Westminster Abbey, as it possesses a fine choir.

EGERTON. Can there be any doubt where Christian duty lies in this matter? Through the grace of our Lord, Jesus Christ. Amen.

CONGREGATION. *(Off. Simultaneous with EGERTON.)* Amen.

*(He leaves the pulpit. SUSANNAH and HANDEL are in Mary's salon, reminiscing happily.)*

HANDEL. Dublin threw its arms open to her, Mrs. Pendarves.

SUSANNAH. Yes, after you told it to. *(Mimicking HANDEL.)* "This woman has the voice of the angel, Gabriel. You come hear her sing, it will make you better."

HANDEL. It did make them better. When I found her, she was doing bad plays with no singing. I rescued her and put her in my oratorio.

MARY. Bravo!

SUSANNAH. Oh, Mary, it was wonderful. I went to parties! And I laughed — and I bought gowns! And I sang!

HANDEL. Now you will do the same here.

SUSANNAH. Herr Handel, you will stand by me?

HANDEL. Now I am what, a post which you lean on? You will be a triumph.

SUSANNAH. *(Wanting to believe.)* Do you think so?
HANDEL. I am Handel. I don't think. I know.
SUSANNAH. *(Now she is convinced and radiantly happy.)* Yes.
Alright, then. London at last! Oh, I can feel Molly in my arms!

*(They disappear as SMITH comes on, places a manuscript on JENNENS'S table and leaves, all in one action.)*

SMITH. Mr. C. Jennens, esquire. Dear sir: I have the honor of presenting to you the orchestrations for *Messiah,* which is to receive its London premiere in Handel's upcoming season at Covent Garden.

*(As SMITH leaves, JENNENS eagerly turns to read the manuscript. He is immediately disappointed.)*

JENNENS. Damnation! An overture!

*(EGERTON is again at the pulpit.)*

EGERTON. Now I should like to invite to this pulpit a lay person with profound spiritual strength and insight, gained through suffering for the sake of the faith.

*(As JENNENS disappears, KITTY comes to the pulpit, looking as pious as it is possible for her to look.)*

KITTY. I am Mrs. Catherine Clive, a name with which many of you are doubtless familiar, due to my classical acting at Drury Lane. It is my sad duty to relate to you a small portion of my sufferings at the hands of the composer whose new oratorio none of us will be attending. When I sang operas for him — a period lost to the town's memory, I thank God, as I sang under an assumed Italian name — he routinely mistreated me. "Sing better, damn you!" he frequently bellowed into me face. When on one occasion I offered my opinion that his opera, *Alcina,* might offend the God-fearing of the town, he tried to throw me out the window of his salon — even though I was singing the third-act aria like an angel. He raged — and I quote — "I will throw your ass out the window!" Or some such words. I still shake at the memory. And in Ireland he chose to employ for his singing a woman whose infamy is so deep, it does no good to hide her name which is Susannah Cibber. We all know the shame she brought upon herself and the town, which it does no Christian good to contemplate. And, moreover, she is not even a good singer. Through Jesus Christ, Our Lord. Amen.

*(KITTY is now the still point around which activity turns. The table is replaced, the chair held out for her as she sits.)*

### Scene Two
*Offstage Dressing Area, Drury Lane Theatre*
*The next evening*

*(HANDEL enters.)*

HANDEL. Ah, there you are, Mrs. Clive! I find you at last. What classical role do you play tonight — Hamlet?

KITTY. What are you doing here? It seems anyone may come backstage at Drury Lane now!

HANDEL. I have come to offer you a job.

KITTY. What!?

HANDEL. I wish for you to sing for me this season at Covent Garden. Do not worry. I will arrange with Fleetwood so the public does not miss any of your captivating performances here.

KITTY. Get out, you — you pig!

HANDEL. Ach! Again with the pig. What is wrong?

KITTY. I will not be made sport of in me own theatre!

HANDEL. I am making no sport, I assure you. I would not come to this temple of mediocrity just for sport. I came also last week to hear you sing. Polly from *Beggar's Opera*. You did not know that, did you?

KITTY. No.

HANDEL. You have a fine voice, I find, Mrs. Clive. I wish it to sing in the London performance of *Messiah*. Will it?

KITTY. You're serious? You don't want me to act out bloody Ophelia's bleedin' loony scene first?

HANDEL. No, no, I assure you, I am in complete earnest.

KITTY. How do I know that?

HANDEL. I do not engage singers as a joke, Mrs. Clive.

KITTY. Oh. Well then. Pray, do call me Kitty.

HANDEL. Will you come sing for me, Kitty?

KITTY. Well, if you're truly in earnest — *(Suddenly remembering.)* Oh Lord, wait. Damn.

HANDEL. What? I have already spoken to Fleetwood, I told you.

KITTY. No, it's ... Well, this is bleedin' awkward. Oh, well, you'll hear it from someone, so you may as well hear it from me, I suppose. But I assure you, I meant no real offense.

HANDEL. Why, Kitty, whatever are you saying?

KITTY. Do you ever go to St. Paul's, Mr. Handel?

HANDEL. Surely. I was there yesterday for matins.

KITTY. What!

HANDEL. *(Really enjoying this.)* "When I sang operas for him, he shouted, 'Sing better, damn you!'" So, Kitty, what Italian name did you assume during the shrouded period of our past collaboration? Wait! It comes back to me! It was Kittini, wasn't it?

KITTY. *(HANDEL laughs through this.)* You mustn't think, Mr. Handel ... it was Henry Egerton who convinced me to do it. Oh, do stop laughing!

*(It may be that KITTY, herself, can't quite keep from giggling a little.)*

HANDEL. *(Still vastly amused.)* "And I quote — 'I will throw your ass out the window!'" Oh dear, oh dear. When you said that, one woman in the back of the nave dropped her knitting!

KITTY. Shh! They'll hear you onstage.

HANDEL. *(Finally subsides.)* Listen, you were angry with me; you had your joke. What does it matter? We are professionals. So you will sing for me?

KITTY. Yes!

HANDEL. Good. I'll tell Dubourg and Mrs. Cibber. Come to my

house tomorrow at noon, please.

KITTY. Susannah Cibber is singing for you?

HANDEL. You knew this. You said so in your sermon.

KITTY. But only in Ireland. Surely her voice isn't good enough for your music here.

HANDEL. She will sing the notes on the page. As, I trust, will you. She will stand beside you as mezzo in *Messiah*.

KITTY. I? A Christian woman? Stand beside Susannah Cibber? I have me reputation to think of, Mr. Handel.

HANDEL. Come, Kitty. Do you not think your anger goes on too long? Come, sing with Susannah.

KITTY. *(Very unhappy.)* I'll be damned if I sing with Susannah Cibber!

HANDEL. Ach. Goodbye, then, Mrs. Clive.

*(He leaves.)*

KITTY. Oh ... *(She cannot think of a word terrible enough.)* Oh!

### Scene Three
*St. Paul's Cathedral, Evensong*
*The Salon of Handel's House, Brook Street*
*March 17/19*

*(EGERTON is again at the pulpit.)*

EGERTON. I have received from a learned friend a letter which will be printed in the *Spectator* in two days' time. He writes, *(Reads)* "An oratorio either is an act of religion, or it is not; if it is, I ask if the playhouse is a fit temple to perform it in, or players fit ministers of God's word? If it is performed for amusement, what a profanation of God's name and word is this, to make so light use of them!"

*(HANDEL and KITTY have stayed on. Now KITTY is practicing "How beautiful are the feet" from <u>Messiah</u>, HANDEL playing the occasional note on the harpsichord to guide her. Her singing*

*and EGERTON'S preaching run together.)*

KITTY. *(Sings)* "How beautiful are the feet of them that preach the gospel of peace."

EGERTON. My friend chooses to edify the town anonymously, and so signs his letter, "Philalethes."

KITTY. *(Sings)* "How beautiful are the feet, how beautiful are the feet of them that preach the gospel of peace."

EGERTON. Most disturbing of all is the woman, Cibber, who means to sing in it. It is as though the Whore of Babylon were to stand shamelessly naked before us all in this cathedral church and recite the Lord's Prayer.

KITTY. *(Sings)* "How beautiful are the feet of them that preach the gospel of peace."

EGERTON. Handel means to perform his sacrilege in six days' time. It is, therefore, now the moment for us to be counted for Christ's soldiers. And I say that whoever finds and removes notices for *Messiah* does nothing but service to God! *(He starts to leave the pulpit; then, as an afterthought:)* Ah. And let us continue to pray for the wayward soul of Mrs. Catherine Clive.

*(EGERTON exits.)*

KITTY. *(Sings)* "And bring glad tidings, and bring glad tidings, glad tidings of good things."

*(Something in the aria has struck KITTY and she has become a little emotional towards the end. HANDEL notices.)*

HANDEL. Kitty, is there something wrong?
KITTY. Can't I like a song?
HANDEL. Of course. Now we will practice "Rejoice greatly."
KITTY. No, we won't! I can sing it in me sleep! Now, listen, Mr. Handel. "He shall feed his flock" is a soprano aria, and I want it. You wrote it for my register, not bloody Susannah Cibber's.
HANDEL. I will transpose it down for her.
KITTY. It's not fair! You already gave her "If God be for us"!

Look, she's got "O thou that tellest," "He was despised," "Thou art
gone up," "If God be for us," and "Oh death, where is thy sting?"

KITTY. And I've only got "But who may abide," "Rejoice
greatly," "But thou didst not leave," "How beautiful are the feet," and
"I know that my Redeemer liveth."

HANDEL. So?

KITTY. So, that's six for her and five for me — if you give her
"He shall feed his flock."

HANDEL. Ah, but you have "And lo, the angel of the Lord," and
"There were shepherds abiding."

KITTY. Those are recitatives, thank you, not arias.

HANDEL. I am not sure I believe I am having this conversation.

KITTY. Look, just because you stole soprano songs for her in
Ireland don't mean you can do it to me! She will not have more songs
than me or I won't sing! *(HANDEL suddenly laughs.)* What's so
amusing, may I ask?

HANDEL. Oh, Kittini! You are an absurd woman! But, still, I am
glad you changed your mind. It is good to have you with us!

KITTY. Well, don't you look like the cat what swallowed the
bleedin' canary!

HANDEL. The what? What swallowed the what? This is
English?

KITTY. Bloody foreigner! It means, you look uncommonly
pleased with yourself!

HANDEL. Ah, yes, I am! I knew you would come.

KITTY. Well, I couldn't spend me whole life standing next to
Henry Egerton at St. Paul's Cathedral. Besides, do you know what I
found out? They don't pay a farthing for singing in church!

HANDEL. *(He knows this, of course.)* No? This is an outrage!

*(SUSANNAH breezes in.)*

SUSANNAH. Am I late, Herr Handel?

HANDEL. No, come in, come in. We are just speaking of cats
and canaries.

SUSANNAH. *(Sees KITTY.)* Oh, I beg your pardon. I did not

think you would still be here.

KITTY. Just making me departure. *(Preparing to go.)* Mr. Handel. *(Icily)* Mrs. Cibber.

SUSANNAH. *(Equally frosty.)* Mrs. Clive.

HANDEL. Oh, you are babies! Both of you! You are worse than Cuzzoni and Faustina — and this takes some doing. Cuzzoni once attacked Faustina with a hatpin. But at least they would rehearse together in the same room.

SUSANNAH. I have no objection, Herr Handel, as you know.

KITTY. No, you wouldn't, dear. You'll be in the same room with anybody.

SUSANNAH. *(To HANDEL.)* Shall we begin?

HANDEL. Yes, by all means. Fare you well, Mrs. Clive, if off you must go.

KITTY. Now you remember what I said, about "He shall feed his flock."

SUSANNAH. What about, "He shall feed his flock"?

HANDEL. Oh, no.

KITTY. That's my song now.

SUSANNAH. Herr Handel? I sang it in Dublin.

HANDEL. Yes. It was too high for you —

KITTY. It needs a real soprano, dear, not someone with a one-octave range —

HANDEL. — and so, as I have told our Kittini, I will transpose it down for you. B flat major to F major. Easy as pie.

SUSANNAH. *(Nettled)* Perhaps you should not, if you believe it falls more naturally into Mrs. Clive's considerable range. Perhaps she would do the aria better justice.

KITTY. Exactly.

HANDEL. I have said what we shall do.

KITTY. I WILL NEVER YIELD "HE SHALL FEED HIS FLOCK!" And, what is more, I won't be seen on the Covent Garden stage next to this woman. John Beard and Tom Lowe and the two basses must stand between us.

SUSANNAH. That suits me right down to the ground! Standing next to you, Mrs. Clive, I might be mistaken for one of the lower animals.

KITTY. *(All of KITTY's dislike of SUSANNAH boils over into a physical assault.)* You feigning, canting bitch!
SUSANNAH. Damn you to hell, Kitty Clive!

*(They fight. HANDEL attempts to intervene. SMITH enters.)*

SMITH. What on earth — ?
HANDEL. We are rehearsing. *(To the women.)* Stop! You must stop! Help me, Smith — they are sopranos! *(SMITH helps HANDEL pull the women apart.)* Now, you will please sit and breathe slowly and think happy, pleasant thoughts for a few moments.

*(They sit in chairs, well apart from each other.)*

KITTY. *(Shocked)* You choked me!
SUSANNAH. *(Surprised, herself.)* Yes. Sorry.
HANDEL. I beg you, neither of you, to leave now. We must resolve this war between you —
SUSANNAH. It is her war, Herr Handel. I have never done the woman injury —
KITTY. No? Tell that to me poor, wrung neck!
SUSANNAH. — until now.
HANDEL. Please, I am asking as a great favor that we settle the bad blood between you. Now —

*(But JENNENS enters, angry. He takes no notice of the women, makes straight for HANDEL. He has just come down from Gopsal.)*

JENNENS. Damn you, Handel! It is unconscionable! How could you treat my libretto so?
HANDEL. Mr. Jennens, how are you, sir? The ladies and I are attempting to resolve —
JENNENS. You have ruined my scripture collection!
HANDEL. You have not even heard the music!
JENNENS. Smith sent me a copy.

*(He produces it.)*

HANDEL. Smith!

SMITH. He *is* the librettist.

JENNENS. I specifically said, no overture! And what do I find? Measure after measure of overture!

KITTY. Who's this, then?

SMITH. Not now, Mrs. Clive, please.

HANDEL. You said, it's an opera. An opera needs an overture.

JENNENS. And another sinfony in the middle!

HANDEL. Ah, yes, the pastoral. Bach used one in his Christmas cantata.

JENNENS. You are not Bach! And you changed my text! Look! "How beautiful are the feet." I used the scripture from Romans. You changed it to one from Isaiah!

HANDEL. So? They are both about feet! Isaiah was more musical.

JENNENS. The whole thing was composed in too much haste! This music is not worthy of my text! You must rewrite!

HANDEL. How can I? We perform in four days. As you say, I am not Bach!

SUSANNAH. They loved it in Ireland, Mr. Jennens.

JENNENS. Ireland! Filthy Papists and yokels! This is London. Look at your orchestrations, Handel. They're simple-minded! A few strings and a harpsichord!

HANDEL. There is also a trumpet!

JENNENS. And you copied yourself! All through this are tunes I have heard before — that everyone has heard before! The "O death" aria is from one of your damned Italian duets! And not all these tunes are even yours!

SMITH. Now, Mr. Jennens.

HANDEL. I am not some amateur dabbler with all his living paid on a country estate in Leicestershire!

SMITH. Handel!

HANDEL. Understand. I write song after song, concerto after anthem after oratorio — all at breakneck speed — just to survive the town's mania for new things! When I am fortunate enough to create a melody of quality, I keep it in my head and use it again somewhere else. And yes, sometimes I find a tune from Scarlatti or someone, and improve upon it. Other composers also borrow from me. It is how we all manage.

JENNENS. Never again! I had as soon *Messiah* not perform as that it be performed thus!

*(He tosses his copy on the floor. HANDEL picks it up, reverently.)*

HANDEL. *(Quietly)* You wrong this work.

SMITH. You may have your wish, Mr. Jennens. *(Produces a Spectator and gives it to HANDEL.)* Another anonymous letter-writer. Philalethes he calls himself. Philalethes?

JENNENS. Lover of truth.

HANDEL. Let me see. *(Reads)* "The Old Testament is not to be profaned alone, but the New must be joined with it." Smith, this Philalethes, he has not even seen *Messiah!* How can he condemn?

JENNENS. Perhaps he has got wind of the music.

SMITH. It doesn't matter. They are tearing down your notices all over town. We cannot afford another failure. And we cannot have the town against us again. The last London saw of you was ranting at Lincoln's Inn Fields.

HANDEL. *(Reads)* "How must it offend to hear the most sacred name of Messiah sung by a set of people very unfit."

KITTY. I beg his pardon. We are not all of us unfit.

*(SUSANNAH stands.)*

SUSANNAH. No. He means me. I'm sure of it.

JENNENS. Well, madam, what *will* London think, I wonder, when it hears holy scripture issue from your mouth?

SMITH. Mr. Jennens!

SUSANNAH. He's right. No one wishes to hear a possibly still syphilitic whore sing "If God be for us, who can be against us." I am the stain on *Messiah*. Remove me and it will be pure again. Herr Handel, what shall I do? What do you wish me to do? *(No one will meet her gaze, least of all HANDEL, who is still stunned by what he has read in the Spectator.)* Oh. *(Suddenly knowing no one wants her to stay, she quickly gathers her things to go.)* I shall remove myself. Kitty can sing my parts. No doubt she has already learned them.

*(SUSANNAH runs from the room. A moment or two of stunned silence.)*

SMITH. She may be right.

HANDEL. *(Very quietly.)* Are we all cowards?

KITTY. Well, actually, I *have* learned her parts.

*(SMITH becomes the still point now. All disappear except him.)*

### Scene Four
*The salon of Mary Pendarves's house*
*Later that day*

*(MARY enters, very agitated — but remembering her good manners. She ricochets in tone between her anxiety and her duty as a hostess.)*

MARY. We must find her, Mr. Smith! Do have some tea.

SMITH. Thank you. Handel is still out inquiring for her.

MARY. I shall send my man again. Sugar?

SMITH. No, thank y —. *(In her agitated state, she plops it in without waiting for SMITH's reply.)* Thank you.

MARY. Nay, I shall go myself! Cream?

SMITH. No. *(She adds it.)* Thank you. Really, Mrs. Pendarves, what can be done is being done. Handel fears now she may have quit the town.

MARY. Oh, my poor Susannah! Gin?

SMITH. *(He covers his glass to prevent this addition.)* Do sit down, Mrs. Pendarves. *(She sits.)* The performance is now in some doubt.

MARY. But I understand the Clive woman —

SMITH. Yes, she can sing Mrs. Cibber's parts — and believes she can sing the tenor and bass parts, too — and probably the choruses.

MARY. What then?

SMITH. There is much opposition in the town. They're tearing down Handel's notices.

    MARY. Who is?

    SMITH. Who indeed? Philalethes, I suppose.

    MARY. But surely Philalethes is only a few crotchety bishops. Do they know the concert is for charity?

    SMITH. It's difficult to gauge the extent of the animosity.

    MARY. Then it's as I feared. Drastic action is called for. To arms, Mr. Smith!

    SMITH. I beg your pardon.

    MARY. I employ a military metaphor.

    SMITH. Ah, well then, I fear retreat is more in order.

    MARY. No, no! I have responded to this Philalethes fellow.

*(Takes out her letter.)*

    SMITH. Oh, yes?

    MARY. In verse! You shall determine if my reply is sufficient to crush the enemy. *(Reads)* "Wrote extempore by a gentleman, on reading the *Spectator*." One writes in disguise, you see.

    SMITH. Very wise.

    MARY. *(Reads) "On Mr. Handel's New Oratorio."*
"Cease, zealot, cease to blame these heavenly lays,
And demanding only angels sing Messiah's praise!
Don't you find, Mr. Smith, that there is nothing quite so rebuking as stinging verses, well laid on? They are like a cavalry charge!

    SMITH. Well —

    MARY. *(Reads)*
"Handel's hallowed songs give to music new grace,
And at the theatre, they sanctify the place;
To exalt the meanest singer, and make of Hell a Heaven."
Well, Mr. Smith, what do you think?

    SMITH. You are saying Covent Garden is Hell?

    MARY. But made into Heaven by Handel's music. Is it an apt reply? Will it capture the town again for the Master? I mean to send it immediately to the *Daily Advertiser*.

    SMITH. I cannot say.

    MARY. Can't you? Well. You shall see. And now, Mr. Smith, prepare for my second fusillade! *(Taking out another piece of paper.)*

*Messiah,* as a title, seems rather to raise the hair on the backs of the bishops' necks. So, we fire a new title at them!

SMITH. *(Taking the paper and examining it with approval.)* Do you know, that's rather good. Bullseye, Mrs. Pendarves!

*(SUSANNAH comes on, dressed for travel, but, this time, with only a small bag. She is waiting for the coach.)*

### Scene Five
*Coach stop by an inn on the Dover Road*
*Evening of the same day*

*(SMITH and MARY disappear as SUSANNAH waits by the road.)*

VOICE. *(Recorded)* Reading your record of response, members of the jury, I see you find William Sloper guilty of adultery. This court chooses to restrict its punishment to a fine of, shall we say, £1 sterling? Since no actual harm was done the woman.

HANDEL. *(Entering and seeing her.)* Waiting for the coach. I should have known it would be so. What are you playing at? I told you. I will transpose down the aria.

SUSANNAH. You know it isn't the aria.

HANDEL. I must warn you, Mrs. Cibber. My feet hurt. I have been searching for you all day. So now please come.

SUSANNAH. Herr Handel —

HANDEL. Stop! I do not wish to hear anything which will upset me. You are a singer; you must sing.

SUSANNAH. They won't let me. Before I even step onto the stage, the whispering will start. Then the sniggering and the jeering…

HANDEL. No, this is only your fantasy.

SUSANNAH. I will not face all that again.

HANDEL. You must come back. Otherwise you are a coward!

SUSANNAH. Then so are you. You're frightened to the top of your head.

HANDEL. What!

SUSANNAH. Why didn't you stop me? When I left your salon? You're afraid I'll drag your oratorio into the mud. Admit it.

HANDEL. Do not make me angry!

SUSANNAH. *(Losing her temper.)* Oh, why not! Everything makes you angry! Be angry!

HANDEL. How dare you!

SUSANNAH. Live up to your bloody reputation.

HANDEL. Who else gives you the chance to go on stage in London?

SUSANNAH. Well, I don't want the chance!

HANDEL. Then you *are* a coward! And also a traitor! And — Oh, I cannot think of words bad enough for you!

SUSANNAH. How about "person very unfit"? How about whore? Say it!

HANDEL. No.

SUSANNAH. Why not? And then perhaps you'll wish to strike me.

HANDEL. Strike you?

SUSANNAH. Theophilus used to do it. Go on. Break my jaw! I deserve it, don't I?

HANDEL. Oh, no. No, Susannah.

SUSANNAH. Go on! Angry Handel! Handel Furioso!

*(This deflates HANDEL utterly. It takes him a moment to recover.)*

HANDEL. Ach, you are right. I was afraid, as you said. Of the mud and the jeers. And also that my music they jeer again. I was not a good post.

SUSANNAH. What?

HANDEL. You know, which you lean on. I'm sorry.

SUSANNAH. It doesn't matter now.

HANDEL. It does matter. I feel ashamed.

SUSANNAH. Yes. It's awful, isn't it? It's what I feel every time my heart beats, every time I breathe.

HANDEL. But Susannah, in Ireland everyone adored you. You sang like a seraph.

SUSANNAH. I managed it there for awhile. But this place wants to be rid of me.

HANDEL. I don't want to be rid of you.

SUSANNAH. Well, you ought to. I'm going to France.

HANDEL. France? Why not to Molly?

SUSANNAH. I didn't fix my reputation.

HANDEL. Susannah, listen to me. No, you must listen. When I first read Mr. Jennens' libretto, I saw a part about Christ. He was despised and rejected. And I thought, yes, this is like me: I have given the town my soul and they have scourged it and they have never said sorry to me once. Suddenly I wanted to write again, to pour out my anger. And in my score I would put a secret. That it would be about me. Handel Furioso.

SUSANNAH. Oh.

HANDEL. But then, I had a sort of vision. I saw you, Susannah.

SUSANNAH. Me?

HANDEL. Yes. Who also has been a little despised. And rejected and acquainted with grief. Remember? You sang it in Ireland.

SUSANNAH. Yes.

HANDEL. I wrote it for you. And for the king, so lonely now. And maybe even for my enemies who make such bad music. Finally I understood. It is not your little life, Handel. It is everyone's. Everyone has had their hearts broken. Come. Sing the aria tonight.

SUSANNAH. I told you —

HANDEL. Yes, yes. The sniggering. Do not sing it for them. Sing it for you.

SUSANNAH. That's a dream. All of it. Going on stage. Having Molly. I must finally learn to bear my life, my real life.

HANDEL. Singing tonight, maybe that is your real life. Even with the sniggers. Maybe that is God's purpose for you.

SUSANNAH. God's purpose? Do you really believe in that?

HANDEL. Yes. But then, I drink a lot of port.

SUSANNAH. I don't believe in God's purpose.

HANDEL. I know this. It is why you wait for the Dover coach. I too have waited here, you know. Oh yes. When an opera fails or someone writes "Handel the German pig" in a newspaper, I come here. I think about going to Halle, my birth town, with its linden trees, and cry a little about this cold country.

SUSANNAH. But never take the coach?

HANDEL. Always I watch it go past.

SUSANNAH. If I come back and sing, it could ruin your oratorio. It might very well ruin you.

HANDEL. So? In that case, we will just come back here. There is always a coach going to Dover.

SUSANNAH. I can't … change my life.

HANDEL. No, you are right. Only what comes next.

SUSANNAH. *(Standing)* Is that the coach?

HANDEL. Susannah, tell me this. All you have suffered, your heartbreak. Where is its purpose? What will be its meaning now? Yes, you are right. Here is your coach coming. Shall I get out my handkerchief and wave goodbye?

### Scene Six
#### Audience Chamber, St. James's Palace
#### March 23

*(As SUSANNAH and HANDEL disappear, the KING enters and sits at the table. He reads a book. EGERTON enters.)*

GEORGE II. Ah, Bishop! Come in. Thank you for coming. I am happy to see you.

EGERTON. *(Surprised)* You are?

GEORGE II. It seems this fellow, John Locke — he was not a beeist, as you supposed. He was an Anglican. How could you have got it wrong?

EGERTON. I beg your pardon, sir?

GEORGE II. I have been reading!

EGERTON. Your Majesty!

GEORGE II. *Ja, ja,* it is very interesting.

EGERTON. May I? *(The KING gives the book to him.)* "An Essay Concerning Human Understanding." John Locke. Do you find the book edifying, your Majesty?

GEORGE II. *(Chuckles)* You mean, do I understand it?

EGERTON. Forgive me, your Majesty, I do not wish to offend.

GEORGE II. No, go ahead and offend, Bishop. I value your thoughts on these things.

EGERTON. I believe, as I'm certain you do, that the will of God is paramount. Did Locke? He is ambivalent on the subject. Which is why he is so dangerous to the faith. Oh, he pretended to devoutness, but he undermined from within. The Devil may appear as an angel of light, sir. His kind are much worse than someone like, oh, Thomas Hobbes.

GEORGE II. Hobbes?

EGERTON. Another philosopher of the last century. A professed atheist.

GEORGE II. *(Writing the name.)* Thomas Hobbes. Thank you, Bishop. You are educating me something marvelous.

EGERTON. *(This is not the result he had intended.)* No, no —

GEORGE II. You may go back to your sermons now, Bishop.

EGERTON. If I might take this opportunity, your Majesty?

GEORGE II. *Ja,* go on.

EGERTON. *(He produces new playbill for Messiah.)* Please look at this.

GEORGE II. *(He examines it.)* So? Another oratorio by Handel.

EGERTON. No, sir, it is the same. It merely has a new title.

GEORGE II. *"A New Sacred Oratorio."* Hmm. Not very catchy.

EGERTON. He takes off the title, *Messiah* and substitutes the word, "sacred," to draw in the devout. This oratorio is a species of devil appearing as an angel of light.

GEORGE II. Ah, Bishop, but what if it really were an angel?

EGERTON. Your Majesty?

GEORGE II. What if this oratorio were not a devil, but a real angel.

EGERTON. Well, then, of course, it would behoove the devout to embrace it, but —

GEORGE II. And you? What about you?

EGERTON. Me, your Majesty?

GEORGE II. *Ja, ja.* Would you embrace it?

EGERTON. So long as we are speaking in the subjunctive mood, sir, then yes, I would. But, alas, I have not discovered that when oratorios perform, Eucharist attendance increases at St. Paul's.

GEORGE II. *(Looks at the playbill.)* And Handel's oratorio performs for the first time tonight.

EGERTON. At Covent Garden Theatre. We have done our best to awaken the town to its blasphemy, but —

GEORGE II. But. You have something you wish me to do.

EGERTON. Yes, your Majesty. Close the theatre.

GEORGE II. What!

EGERTON. Close Covent Garden Theatre tonight. Do not let Handel's oratorio do its damage to this Christian town.

GEORGE II. I cannot do this.

EGERTON. *(Produces document.)* But you can! The theatres function by royal patent. You grant them; you can rescind them. This has been true since the time of Charles II.

GEORGE II. Hmmph. A Stuart King. Did he ever close a theatre?

EGERTON. He most certainly did, sir. *(Shows document.)* Look —

GEORGE II. No, you do not understand me. *I* cannot do this. We are done in England with all this high-handed Stuart nonsense. Walpole and Parliament rule this country.

EGERTON. But I am trying to say, you have the right —

GEORGE II. The right? Oh! Because it says so on your piece of paper? Your King in the old days — Henry the Ninth —

EGERTON. The Eighth, I think. Sorry.

GEORGE II. *Ja, ja,* the Eighth. He had the right to cut off his wives' heads. It said so on a piece of paper. Which he wrote! This is tyranny! The House of Hanover is not a tyrant! Go to Parliament and get them to write a bill to close your theatre.

EGERTON. I ... tried.

GEORGE II. Well?

EGERTON. They dithered.

GEORGE II. *Ja.* Dithering is the price we pay for no tyranny.

EGERTON. But, your Majesty, this is a very particular case. I implore you, with all the energy of my heart. Please consider it.

*(He holds out the manuscript, which the KING reluctantly takes.)*

GEORGE II. *Ja,* Bishop, alright. I will consider. But I wonder, would the Queen have enjoyed this oratorio? She was so thrilled by *Saul.*

EGERTON. I ... cannot say.

GEORGE II. No. You cannot. *(EGERTON bows to leave. The*

*KING eyes the* <u>Messiah</u> *notice suspiciously.)* Bishop. Was this notice torn down?

EGERTON. Alas, one cannot always curb the zeal of one's parishioners.

### Scene Seven
#### Outside Covent Garden Theatre
#### That evening

*(As EGERTON and the KING disappear, MARY hurries to the door of Covent Garden Theatre. SMITH follows.)*

SMITH. Mrs. Pendarves! Do wait, madam!

MARY. I fear we shall be late!

SMITH. The performance is not for an hour. Even Handel has not yet arrived.

MARY. Ah, here we are. When they attack, one is bound to say it will be here.

SMITH. At the front door to the theatre?

MARY. Where else? It is the portcullis behind which the Master's music lies. Another military metaphor.

SMITH. For the life of me, I cannot conceive what attack you anticipate.

MARY. From the clergy, of course! The brutes of the cloth! Not my own dear priest at St. George's, of course. He has bought his ticket and will sit in the theatre like a Christian. No, I speak of the rougher, hooligan element of the Church. Bishops and above.

SMITH. But Mrs. Pendarves —

MARY. One is shocked to discover them ruffians, but there it is. At any moment a brigade of bishops will appear with sword and fire, their faces hideously smeared with pitch.

SMITH. For what purpose?

MARY. To overwhelm us, to capture this theatre and prevent tonight's performance!

SMITH. No, no, I assure you —

MARY. I assure *you*, sir! The things said against the Master and poor Susannah have been incendiary!

SMITH. Well, what do you propose to do, then, against an assault of bishops?

MARY. I am armed, as you see!

*(Produces paper.)*

SMITH. Your poem for the *Advertiser.*

MARY. I shall read my stinging verses out to them at full voice!

SMITH. You intend to attack them with poetry?

MARY. This surely will repulse them.

SMITH. That's dashed brave, Mrs. Pendarves, but I think the clergy will not arrive. They don't need to, you see. They have so prejudiced the town against Handel that few will come tonight. They've already won, I'm afraid.

MARY. Well, Mr. Smith, you must believe what you will.

SMITH. We may as well go in, since we're here.

MARY. Please believe me, Mrs. Pendarves —

*(EGERTON arrives, with some notices and a hammer and nails. MARY sees him first.)*

MARY. Put down your weapon, sir!

SMITH. *(Seeing the BISHOP.)* Crikey!

EGERTON. I must ask you good people to stand away from this door.

MARY. Will you surrender your weapon?

EGERTON. It's a hammer, madam. I am his Majesty's Clerk of the Closet, here on his Majesty's business.

MARY. And where are the rest of you?

EGERTON. I beg your pardon?

MARY. Where are your fellow Visigoths in priestly garb?

SMITH. She was expecting a brigade with sword and fire.

EGERTON. I have notices to attach to this building.

MARY. Very well, you have been warned. *(Reads)*
"Cease, zealot, cease to blame these heavenly lays,
And demanding only angels sing Messiah's praise!"

EGERTON. Is this woman sane?

MARY. "Nor, for your trivial argument, opine, 'The theatre is not fit for praise divine!'" I added that couplet.

SMITH. It's rather good.

MARY. Do you think so? *(Reads)* "Handel's hallowed songs gives to music new grace —"

EGERTON. Oh, really, madam!

*(He snatches the poem.)*

MARY. Brute! Ruffian!

SMITH. Steady on, Bishop.

EGERTON. What sort of rot is this? *(Looking the poem over.)* Ah, yes. You are one of these Handel idolaters. You are one who loves an aria more than the commandments of God.

MARY. One is bound to say, I never knew them to be incompatible.

EGERTON. Your spiritual senses have been deadened by all this theatre music. You hear a soprano sing a top note and think you are hearing the voice of God.

MARY. You are uncommonly vulgar, sir. Even for a Bishop.

*(EGERTON gives copies of his notice to MARY and SMITH. SMITH examines his closely.)*

EGERTON. His Majesty has revoked the patent for this theatre. You see, madam, I need neither sword nor fire to close Covent Garden; I have the law. Now, if you will be so kind?

*(He means, get out of my way.)*

SMITH. I believe we must do as he says. I'm sorry.

MARY. No.

*(She tears the notice EGERTON has given her in half.)*

EGERTON. What you have just done is a breach of the law. Now stand aside.

MARY. I shall not. Like all men who lack the capacity for art to speak to their souls, you believe it cannot speak to anyone's, that it must all be some sort of fraud. Well I am in full command of all my faculties, Bishop, including the spiritual. I have never mistaken a baritone, let alone a soprano, for the Almighty. I shall stand in the way of your infernal notices so long as my body has the strength to resist. That much, at least, I owe to Handel!

SMITH. Bravo, Mrs. Pendarves! *(To EGERTON.)* What she says goes for me, too, dash it all. In spades.

*(He tears his notice in half, and moves to stand beside MARY.)*

MARY. Eloquently said, Mr. Smith.

EGERTON. You shall be brought into court for this, both of you.

*(HANDEL enters.)*

MARY. Ah, Herr Handel! This Bishop fellow is assaulting your oratorio with filthy notices. But Mr. Smith and I shall not be breached, Shall we, Mr. Smith?

SMITH. *(Not quite understanding her.)* Goodness! I hope not.

EGERTON. This theatre is closed.

HANDEL. No. No. You cannot do this.

EGERTON. I? What is it to do with me? I am merely an instrument.

HANDEL. And you, sir, are out of tune!

*(EGERTON thrusts a notice at him. HANDEL examines it.)*

EGERTON. Whose seal is on this notice?

HANDEL. Why do you dislike my oratorio so? Why? That you quote scripture against it. That you say terrible things against a poor girl who now will not sing.

MARY. Susannah will not sing tonight?

EGERTON. No one will sing tonight. I will not dispute with you. You have read the Philalethes letter, no doubt. It expresses the Church's views exactly.

SMITH. Not the entire Church's views.

MARY. Certainly not. I am in the Church and it is not my view. Nor is it the view of one's well-loved priest at St. George's.

EGERTON. What is this priest's name?

MARY. *(Suddenly worried for him.)* Oh, dear.

HANDEL. Yes, yes, the Philalethes letter. But we all know who is this Philalethes.

EGERTON. I do, yes. I received the letter from his own hands before it was published.

*(JENNENS arrives.)*

HANDEL. Come, Bishop, you are Philalethes! You! The bad-sounding instrument!

*(Hearing the topic of discussion, JENNENS decides to leave, but EGERTON'S speech stops him cold.)*

EGERTON. I certainly am not. Pseudonyms ill become the clergy. One here knows the truth. But will he speak, I wonder.

*(The barest pause before all suddenly know who Philalethes is. Caught out, JENNENS chooses defiance.)*

JENNENS. Yes. I will speak.

HANDEL. Mr. Jennens.

SMITH. You are Philalethes?

MARY. The mind positively boggles.

SMITH. But Philalethes rails against your oratorio!

JENNENS. Against the musical form into which my scripture collection has been cast, yes.

SMITH. *(Almost exploding.)* Well then, why did you importune Handel so to set your dashed scripture collection?

JENNENS. I thought he would write different music! *(Takes out manuscript and turns to a place in the middle.)* Listen. Have you listened to "All we like sheep"? *(Sings)* "All we like sheep —" It sounds like a drinking party! These are sheep that are happy to be astray! You cannot have it both ways. Either a thing is sacred or it is not. My scripture collection is sacred. These — opera tunes — are not.

EGERTON. Exactly so. Our Lord is not the hero of an evening's entertainment. You are dragging God into the mud, Mr. Handel, and the town is losing its very sense of the holy!

HANDEL. But that is exactly where God should be — in the mud!

JENNENS. Herr Handel!

EGERTON. Revolting!

HANDEL. Of course! Listen, Bishop. If you shut God up inside your splendid St. Paul's Cathedral — if you don't let him go outside into the mud and muck of the streets — what hope *is* there for the town? What hope is there for Susannah Cibber? What hope is there for me? God must go into the world, or the world will never be sacred. And you know what? He loves it there! That is the Mystery of Godliness, Mr. Jennens — what you wrote on the front page of *Messiah.*

EGERTON. Go home, Mr. Handel. All of you. And allow me to complete my task.

*(Without warning, the KING arrives.)*

EGERTON. Your Majesty!

GEORGE II. But this is excellent. I thought you would not come.

EGERTON. I — ! How — ? Where are your footmen, sir? Where is all your retinue?

GEORGE II. Shh! *(He pulls him into a confidential clinch.)* I left them at the bottom of the road. I am being discreet.

EGERTON. Yes, your Majesty, but why?

GEORGE II. I come as Defender of the Faith, of course. And now, here you are, too. This is very brave of you, Bishop. It could not be better. We two will listen to this oratorio of Handel's, *ja*? Very closely. And see if it is from the angels or the devils. *(He turns to the others.)* Handel. It has been a long time since I heard your music. Is it any good now?

MARY. It will be ravishing, your Majesty, as always.

GEORGE II. Well, we shall be sitting in the Royal Box and if it offends, as the Bishop fears, be sure we will stop it. In its tracks. And now, we all go in, *ja*? Please, madam. Sirs. Other gentleman who does not bow. Come, come. *(SMITH and JENNENS go in. MARY is behind them. The KING suddenly stops, sees the notice in EGERTON'S hand.)* What is this paper, Bishop?

EGERTON. Ah.

HANDEL. You know nothing of this, your Majesty?

GEORGE II. No.

HANDEL. Really? How intriguing.

EGERTON. I can explain, sir …

HANDEL. These are advertisements for tonight's performance. The Bishop kindly had them printed to replace the ones which were torn down. *(Gently taking the incriminating evidence from EGERTON'S hand.)* Thank you, Bishop. It was most kind of you.

*(He goes in.)*

GEORGE II. *(As they go in.)* Bishop! You surprise me more and more.

### *Scene Eight*
*Backstage, Covent Garden Theatre*
*A few minutes later*

*(As the KING and EGERTON disappear, KITTY enters and the door becomes a table again. She is intently studying the Messiah score, practicing one of her newly acquired parts.)*

KITTY. *(Sings)* "Come unto him, all ye that labor —"

*(SUSANNAH enters, still in her traveling clothes.)*

SUSANNAH. Hello, Kitty.

KITTY. You're like a bad penny, Mrs. Cibber. You do keep showing up.

SUSANNAH. Dubourg's about to tune up the orchestra. We're close to curtain.

KITTY. Yes, so if you don't mind, those of us with work to do had best get to it.

SUSANNAH. Kitty, I want to sing tonight.

KITTY. No! No! Not this time! You left! You bowed out!

SUSANNAH. I'm asking you for my parts back.

KITTY. No! They're mine now! You will not steal parts from me again!

SUSANNAH. It isn't stealing, Kitty. Those parts were mine in Ireland.

KITTY. We're a thousand miles from bleedin' Ireland.

SUSANNAH. Kitty, you have everything. You have Drury Lane and all the leads and Shakespeare —

KITTY. I know what you think of me tragical acting!

SUSANNAH. And now Covent Garden, too. I need this.

KITTY. Let me see. "He lifted up her clothes."

SUSANNAH. And I will have it, Kitty.

KITTY. "Took down his breeches."

SUSANNAH. Oh, go ahead. Recite the whole hateful book. I don't care.

KITTY. Oh, why don't you *leave*?

SUSANNAH. Because I'm a singer. Like you. I didn't especially want to be, but they insisted.

KITTY. Oh, Lord! Don't rehearse it all again.

SUSANNAH. It all turned into misery, but do you know what, Kitty? It also made me into a singer and an actress. If I don't do those things, all the misery will have been for nothing.

KITTY. Got yourself all figured out now, have you? Listen. They'll hiss you right off the stage!

SUSANNAH. Possibly.

KITTY. And you won't get your precious little Molly.

SUSANNAH. You may be right. Probably you are. I still want to sing.

KITTY. Why should I care about that? You don't care about my life, do you?

SUSANNAH. *(She has never thought of this before.)* Yes. Of course.

KITTY. Liar. You can't care about anyone. You're too busy listening to the sound of your own bloody heart breaking.

SUSANNAH. *(Not at all sure of her answer.)* No. That isn't true.

KITTY. Isn't it just! I'm about fed up with your suffering. You walk around like bleedin' Mary Magdalene, and Mr. Handel and his friends feel so sorry for you, while me they treat like a colossal joke. And now here you come. Stealing all me prospects again. *(Beginning to break down.)* What do you think *my* heart's made of, India rubber?

SUSANNAH. Kitty! I never realized —

KITTY. Of course you didn't! You suffering types never do!

SUSANNAH. *(This is a discovery.)* You're right. You truly are. I've thought of nothing but my own troubles for — years.

KITTY. Well, think about mine.

SUSANNAH. Alright.

KITTY. *(Sobbing)* About bloody time.

*(SUSANNAH goes to KITTY, tries to comfort her, but KITTY pulls away, sobbing. SUSANNAH tries one more time, and this time KITTY clings to her.)*

SUSANNAH. Well now, isn't this something? Me actually comforting someone else. Kitty, forgive me, won't you? Finally.

KITTY. For what?

SUSANNAH. I was afraid of Theophilus —

KITTY. Say it.

SUSANNAH. I stole parts from you. I'm sorry. Will you forgive me?

KITTY. No.

SUSANNAH. Listen, Kitty. How about this? You sing *Messiah* tonight. I'll do it some other time. Tonight I shall sit very quietly at the back of the stalls and admire your beautiful voice. Will that reconcile us at last?

KITTY. *(KITTY, still in tears, nods.)* Yes.

SUSANNAH. Well then, good luck, Kitty. I shall clap very loudly for you.

*(She starts to leave.)*

KITTY. No wait! Oh, bleedin' bloody hell! Sodding oratorio!

SUSANNAH. What do you mean?

KITTY. Well: "Come unto him." All that. "With his stripes, we are healed."

SUSANNAH. *(Puzzled)* Yes?

KITTY. Oh, take your bleedin' parts, Susannah. *(Gives them to her.)* If we're to be reconciled, at all, we may as well be reconciled now.

*(SUSANNAH flies into her arms.)*

SUSANNAH. Oh, you *are* good, Kitty, thank you. And I don't think you're coarse.

KITTY. Liar. I still think you're bloody Mary Magdalene.

*(They disappear as the KING and EGERTON, and MARY, SMITH, and JENNENS take their places. The orchestra tunes up.)*

### Scene Nine
#### Royal Box, Gallery, Onstage
#### Covent Garden Theatre
#### A moment later

*(This scene is played presentationally, all characters directly facing the audience. The KING and EGERTON are seated together; MARY, SMITH and JENNENS are seated together; HANDEL, SUSANNAH, and KITTY will be together in the center.)*

GEORGE II. Now then, Bishop, sit well back, please, and do not make a fuss. We are being discreet, *ja*?

EGERTON. Yes, your Majesty.

SMITH. Hang on. I haven't quite caught up. Mr. Jennens, if you hate the music and you hate the singers and you hate the theatre, why on earth are you here?

JENNENS. Well, damn it, it *is my* scripture collection!

*(HANDEL comes out, bows, sits at the harpsichord. Applause.)*

MARY. Look, there's the Master. One wondered if one would every see him bestride his musical steed again!

SMITH. Bestride his what?

MARY. Hush.

*(KITTY and SUSANNAH join HANDEL on the Covent Garden stage.)*

HANDEL. Susannah!
SUSANNAH. Good evening, Herr Handel.
SMITH. Crikey! Look who showed up.
MARY. Oh, my brave Susannah.
HANDEL. Are you —
KITTY. Yes, she is.
HANDEL. Dubourg! Get out the mezzo transpositions.

*(A rising murmur in the audience.)*

GEORGE II. Ah, well, the people have seen me. Now watch, Bishop. This is the one thing the English still like their Kings to do.

*(He stands up, waves majestically. Applause from those onstage, who stand, except JENNENS.)*

SMITH. You must stand, Mr. Jennens. It's the King.
JENNENS. I am a non-juror, sir.

*(The KING sits again, as do the others.)*

GEORGE II. You see? I am more popular by not ruling so much.
MARY. Look, he is about to begin. Oh, blesséd moment. A new work by the Master!

*(HANDEL gives the downstroke to begin the overture. The music continues for some seconds.)*

JENNENS. Why must there be an overture?
SMITH & MARY. Shh.

*(More seconds of music. Then, as though it were now over, applause. Applause marks the transitions between parts of the oratorio, only fragments of which we actually hear. KITTY rises.)*

HANDEL. *(Low voice.)* No, no, this is Susannah's aria. *(SUSANNAH shakes her head, no. HANDEL catches on. In a low voice.)* Dubourg. Back to the B flat.

KITTY. *(Sings)* "Come unto him all ye that labour, come unto him that are heaven laden, and he will give you rest. Take his yoke upon you, and learn of him, for he is meek and lowly of heart, and ye shall find rest unto your souls."

*(Applause. KITTY bows.)*

JENNENS. Brava! Brava, Mrs. Clive!

*(KITTY sits. The music for SUSANNAH's aria begins.)*

GEORGE II. *(To EGERTON, about KITTY.)* She is just this good in *Beggar's Opera.* You should see it some time, Bishop. *(SUSANNAH stands.)* Ah, now it's the Cibber woman again.

EGERTON. Yes.

SUSANNAH. *(Sings)* "He was despised and rejected of men, a man of sorrows, and acquainted with grief."

*(As SUSANNAH sings, EGERTON becomes increasingly absorbed in the music. The KING notices.)*

GEORGE II. Bishop? Are you offended? Shall I … ?

*(EGERTON, completely absorbed, slowly shakes his head no. Now the last instrumental notes of the aria die away and there is a moment of silence. EGERTON finds himself murmuring:)*

EGERTON. Woman, for this may all thy sins be forgiven.

GEORGE II. *(Has he heard right?)* Bishop?

*(Now the applause begins, led by MARY.)*

MARY. Brava, Susannah!

*(Immediately, the Hallelujah Chorus begins, all cast members singing. When they sing, they are no longer quite in character; when they have lines, they are.)*

SUSANNAH, KITTY & CAST. *(Sings)* "Hallelujah, for the Lord God Omnipotent reigneth, Hallelujah!"

*(Singing cuts off, although instrumental accompaniment continues softly. The KING rises, as though seeing a vision.)*

SMITH. Look. The King rises. *(He stands, as do the others, including JENNENS.)* I thought you were a non-juror.
JENNENS. I stand for Handel.
MARY. Bravo, Mr. Jennens!
SUSANNAH, KITTY & CAST. *(Sings)* "Hallelujah, for the Lord God Omnipotent reigneth, Hallelujah!"

*(Singing cuts off as before. SMITH hardly dares to look at the KING.)*

SMITH. He's going to stop it. Poor Handel.
MARY. *(Looking closely at the KING and seeing his mood.)* No. It's something else.
GEORGE II. Bishop! The Queen! I see Caroline! With her angels!
EGERTON. I believe … I may see them, too, your Majesty.
SUSANNAH, KITTY & CAST. *(Sings)* "King of Kings, and Lord of Lords —"

*(Singing and accompaniment cut off, unresolved.)*

### Scene Ten
*Outside the Inn*
*A few days later*

*(All remain onstage, but now HANDEL and SUSANNAH are again at the coach stop. She has slipped her cloak back on.)*

HANDEL. Please give my regards to West Woodhay. You will see Molly?

SUSANNAH. If they let me.

HANDEL. You must try to make them let you. Will you?

SUSANNAH. *(Nods)* Because of you, I think.

*(HANDEL reaches into a pocket to withdraw a small package.)*

HANDEL. Oh, I almost forgot. Here. For her.

SUSANNAH. This is unexpected.

HANDEL. Ach. I have no family here. If I wish to give a little present, then I do.

SUSANNAH. What is it?

HANDEL. A pipe organ. No, it's just a little locket with my picture.

SUSANNAH. *(Surprised at his sentiment.)* Really, Herr Handel? Your picture?

HANDEL. What? You think she would prefer Smith's picture?

SUSANNAH. *(Kissing him on the cheek.)* Thank you. She and I shall treasure it.

HANDEL. So, next season you are with Kitty at Drury Lane?

SUSANNAH. I think so. How about you?

HANDEL. You know Le Blond, my cook? He wants to sing. Well, why not?

SUSANNAH. Why not, indeed? George Frederick Handel can make anyone a singer!

HANDEL. You know you may always sing with me, Susannah. You are most welcome.

SUSANNAH. Then there will be a next season? You will compose?

HANDEL. Ah, look. There is the coach. Let me get out my handkerchief.

SUSANNAH. Herr Handel! What are you playing at? You are ignoring my question. And the coach is still quarter-of-a-mile away.

HANDEL. Ah, but I must go home, where things are waiting for me, yes? *(He waves his handkerchief at her.)* So, goodbye, Mrs. Susannah Cibber. Now I wish to hear all about the bucolic life of West Woodhay. So don't, please, forget to write.

SUSANNAH. I won't, then. I promise. And you, Herr Handel?
HANDEL. Me? Oh, Mrs. Cibber, you know. I never forget to write.

*(And now the chorus thunders to its conclusion.)*

SUSANNAH, KITTY & CAST. "— and he shall reign for ever and ever, Hallelujah!"

*(Blackout)*

# GREAT PLAYWRIGHTS, GREAT PLAYS

| | |
|---|---|
| James Goldman | THE LION IN WINTER |
| Robert Bolt | A MAN FOR ALL SEASONS |
| Neil Simon | PROPOSALS |
| Alan Ayckbourn | COMMUNICATING DOORS |
| Samuel Beckett | ENDGAME |
| Bertolt Brecht | MOTHER COURAGE AND HER CHILDREN |
| Agatha Christie | THE MOUSETRAP |
| Noel Coward | BLITHE SPIRIT |
| Georges Feydeau | A FLEA IN HER EAR |
| Eugene Ionesco | THE BALD SOPRANO |
| David Mamet | THE OLD NEIGHBORHOOD |
| Christopher Hampton | LES LIAISONS DANGEREUSES |
| Dario Fo | WE WON'T PAY! WE WON'T PAY! |
| Athol Fugard | VALLEY SONG |
| George Bernard Shaw | MISALLIANCE |
| Thornton Wilder | OUR TOWN |

*These are among the thousands of plays in Samuel French's*
**BASIC CATALOG OF PLAYS AND MUSICALS**

## *Samuel French, Inc.*
### THE HOUSE OF PLAYS SINCE 1830